AS Business Studies
UNIT 1
2ND EDITION

WOLVERHAMPTON COLLEGE

Module 1: Marketing and Accounting and Finance

John Wolinski

For Yvonne, Lara and Nina for their love, patience and support.

Philip Allan Updates
Market Place
Deddington
Oxfordshire
OX15 0SE

Tel: 01869 338652
Fax: 01869 337590
e-mail: sales@philipallan.co.uk
www.philipallan.co.uk

© Philip Allan Updates 2000
This edition © Philip Allan Updates 2002
ISBN 0 86003 906 4 √ ᏜᏧᎮ

In all cases we have attempted to trace and credit copyright owners of material used.

This Guide has been written specifically to support students preparing for the AQA AS Business Studies Unit 1 examination. The content has been neither approved nor endorsed by AQA and remains the sole responsibility of the author.

Printed by Raithby, Lawrence & Co. Ltd, Leicester

Contents

Introduction

■ ■ ■

Content Guidance

■ ■ ■

Questions and Answers

Introduction

About this guide

This Student Unit Guide has been written with one objective in mind: to provide you with the ideal resource for your revision of AQA Unit 1, AS Business Studies. After this introductory note on the aims and assessment of AS, the guide is divided into two sections: Content Guidance and Questions and Answers.

The first section offers concise coverage of Module 1, combining an overview of key terms and concepts with an identification of opportunities for you to illustrate the higher level skills of analysis and evaluation. The scope for linking different topic areas is also shown.

The second section provides six questions, all focused on a specific area of content and in the same order as the first section. Questions 7 and 8 are integrated Marketing and integrated Finance questions respectively, for final revision purposes. Each question is based on the format of the AS papers and followed by two sample answers (an A-grade and a lower-grade response) interspersed by examiner comments.

You should read through the relevant topic area in the Content Guidance section before attempting the question from the Question and Answer section, and only read the specimen answers after you have tackled the question yourself.

The aims of the AS qualification

AS business studies aims to encourage candidates to:
- develop a critical understanding of organisations, the markets they serve and the process of adding value
- be aware that business behaviour can be studied from the perspectives of a range of stakeholders including customers, managers, creditors, owners/shareholders and employees
- acquire a range of skills, including those involved in decision-making and problem-solving
- be aware of current business structure and practice

Assessment

AS and A2 papers are designed to test certain skills. **Every mark that is awarded on an AS or A2 paper is given for the demonstration of a skill.** The content of the course (the theories, concepts and ideas) provides a framework to allow students to show their skills — recognising the content on its own is not enough to merit high marks.

The following skills are tested:
- **Knowledge and understanding** — recognising and describing business concepts and ideas.

- **Application** — being able to explain or apply your understanding.
- **Analysis** — developing a line of thought in order to demonstrate its impact or consequences.
- **Evaluation** — making a judgement by weighing up the evidence provided.

Module 1 (AS Marketing and Accounting and Finance) is weighted so that, on average, marks for each question paper are awarded as follows:

	Weighting	
Knowledge	16/17	how well you know the meanings, theories and ideas
Application	16/17	how well you can explain benefits, problems, calculations, situations
Analysis	12	how well you develop ideas and apply theory and ideas to matters
Evaluation	5*	how well you show judgement, such as the overall significance of the situation
Total	50 marks	

In addition, for Unit 1 there are 2 marks allocated for quality of language.

* In question 1 the evaluation task will include 2 marks for evaluation; in question 2 there will be 3 marks for evaluation — a total of 5 marks in all.

Module 2 (AS People and Operations Management) **and Module 3** (AS External Influences and Objectives and Strategy) have a much higher weighting for the 'higher level' skills of analysis and evaluation. Bear this in mind during your preparation and revision for Modules 2 and 3, as you will need to practise developing arguments more fully for these papers. This will be good practice for the A2 papers that, in general, have a higher weighting for these skills. The units have been designed to allow you to develop these skills as you progress through the course. The examination paper should be weighted so that, on average, marks for each question paper are awarded as follows:

	Weighting	
Knowledge	14/15	how well you know the meanings, theories and ideas
Application	14/15	how well you can explain benefits, problems, calculations, situations
Analysis	12	how well you develop ideas and apply theory and ideas to matters
Evaluation	10/9	how well you show judgement, such as the overall significance of the situation
Total	50 marks	

In addition, for Units 2 and 3 there are 3 marks allocated for quality of language.

The skills requirement of a question

A rough guide to the skills requirement of a question is its mark allocation. In the case of Module 1 (60 minutes), 52 marks are available (including 2 marks for quality of language). After reading the text this is approximately a mark a minute — use this as a guide to the time you spend on each question, but allow some flexibility in your planning. For individual questions the mark allocation is as follows:

2–3 marks a definition or description showing **knowledge**
3–6 marks an explanation or calculation showing **application**
6–8 marks development of an argument in the context of the question showing **analysis**
8–10 marks a judgement of a situation or proposed action showing **evaluation**

In the assessment of 'higher level' questions requiring analysis or evaluation, marks will also be given for the other skills. Factual knowledge displayed, for example, will earn marks for **knowledge** (content) and explanations and calculations will be awarded **application** marks.

A better guide to the skills requirement of a question is to look at the trigger word introducing the question. **Specific trigger words will be used to show you when you are being asked to analyse or evaluate.** For AS, these will be restricted to the following:

Analyse
- 'Analyse...'
- 'Explain why...'
- 'Examine...'

Evaluate
- 'Evaluate...'
- 'Discuss...'
- 'To what extent...?'

If these trigger words are missing on an AS paper, you are being asked to show 'lower level' skills, i.e. knowledge of the specification content or application (explanation).

On the Finance questions, the recall of a formula or method of calculation (e.g. break-even quantity) is knowledge. Carrying out calculations is application. This means that the high mark questions that test analysis and evaluation will not usually involve calculations. Focus on understanding the purposes and limitations of the financial elements of the course and you will be well prepared for these questions. That said, analysis questions may well require you to interpret the meaning of a calculation.

Students who fail to **analyse** generally do so because they have curtailed their argument. The words and phrases below serve to provide logical links in an argument:
- 'and so...'
- 'but in the long run...'
- 'which will mean/lead to...'
- 'because...'

By using them you can demonstrate your ability to analyse. Always ask yourself: 'am I explaining **why**?'

In order to **evaluate**, you need to demonstrate judgement and the ability to reach a reasoned conclusion. The following terms will demonstrate to the examiner that this is your intention:

- 'The most significant...is...because...'
- 'However, ...would also need to be considered because...'
- 'The probable result is...because...'

The suggestions above are only a few of many ways in which judgements can be shown.

Opportunities for evaluation in Module 1

What follows is a summary of many of the probable opportunities for the demonstration of evaluation in Module 1. The structure of the module and the nature of the topics mean that there are more opportunities in the Marketing than in the Finance part of the specification. The list does not include possibilities for evaluation that might arise from combining Marketing and Finance in an evaluative question.

Marketing

- Usefulness of market segmentation/best approach to segmentation.
- Significance of market size, market growth or market share for a company.
- Evaluation of a set of data from a survey.
- Problems based on sampling (size and/or type) and research methods.
- The link between successful (or unsuccessful) marketing and market research.
- The main reasons for the achievement of (or failure to achieve) marketing objectives.
- Judgement based on the relationship between marketing objectives and strategy or mix.
- Recommendations on the use of product differentiation in mass marketing.
- Factors influencing the success of a new entrant.
- Relative merits and demerits of niche marketing.
- Problems of predicting life-cycle stages.
- Usefulness of the concept of product life cycle.
- Usefulness of product portfolio analysis (e.g. through the Boston matrix).
- The best extension strategies.
- The merits of a particular change to the marketing mix.
- The link between successful (or unsuccessful) marketing and a change to one of the four Ps.
- Marketing mix judgements linked to other elements (e.g. market research data or marketing objectives).
- Significance of factors that influence all or particular elements of the marketing mix (e.g. influences on price, promotion, and so on).
- The application of elasticity information to a particular scenario.
- Usefulness of elasticity of demand (price and/or income).

Finance

- Revenue and costs — advice based on simple profit calculations but allowing for other circumstances, possibly the relative balance between fixed and variable costs.
- Usefulness of (static) break-even analysis.
- Best ways to improve cash flow (in given circumstances).
- Decision on whether or not cash flow needs to be improved.
- Discussion of the relative importance of cash flow and profit in a given situation.
- Most appropriate source(s) of finance.
- Best source of finance if limited to internal (or external) finance only.
- Usefulness of budgeting.
- Actions to be taken in response to budget variances.
- Value of delegation of budgets/profit centres.
- Evaluation of whether a financial trend (e.g cash flow or profit) is within a firm's control.

General

Fruitful opportunities for evaluation on any topic are provided by situations in which:

- a link to corporate objectives can be established
- the reliability and completeness of the data can be questioned
- the different views of the stakeholders can be examined

Revision strategies

Below is a list of general pieces of advice for exam preparation.

- Prepare well in advance.
- Organise your files, ensuring there are no gaps.
- Read different approaches — there is no one right approach to business studies. Experience as many views and methods as possible. Read newspapers and business articles.
- When reading an article, try to think of the types of question an examiner might ask and how you would answer them. Remember, some of your examination questions will be based on actual organisations.
- Take notes as you read. These will help you to:
  - put the text into your own words, cementing your understanding
  - summarise and emphasise the key points
  - focus your attention
  - précis information which could help with future revision
  - boost your morale by showing an end product of your revision sessions
- Develop and use your higher level skills. Make sure that your revision is not dominated by factual knowledge only. Check that you can explain and analyse the points noted, and try to imagine situations in which evaluation can be applied.
- Practise examination questions. Use the questions in this book (and past papers if available) to improve your technique, making sure that you complete them in the time allowed. In the examination you must complete two questions in 60 minutes,

so allow 30 minutes per question. Time management is vital. A 60-minute examination paper means that there is limited time to develop answers but you *must* make sure that you have enough time to evaluate the final part of question 2. Remember that, within a question, the later parts carry more marks and therefore need longer, more fully developed answers. All three AS units are marked out of 50 (excluding quality of language marks). After reading time this approximates to 1 mark per minute. Use this as a guide to the time you need to spend on a particular question.

- Maintain your motivation. Reward yourself for achieving targets, but do not get demoralised if you fall behind. If necessary, amend your objectives to a more realistic level.
- Find out the dates and times of your examinations and use this to prepare a detailed schedule for the study leave/examination period, making sure you build in time for relaxation and sleep.
- Focus on all areas of the specification rather than just your favourite topics. Your revision is more likely to 'add value' if it improves your understanding of a problem area. Revising a topic that you already know is a morale booster, but is it as valuable?
- Top up your memory just before the examination. If there are concepts, formulae or ratios that you find difficult, revisit them just before the examination.
- Adopt your own strategy. Everyone has a different learning style — use one that works for you.

Content
Guidance

This section of the guide outlines the topic areas of Module 1 which are as follows:

- Market analysis
- Marketing strategy
- Marketing planning
- Classification of costs, profit, contribution and break-even analysis
- Company accounts
- Budgeting, cost centres and profit centres

Read through the relevant topic area before attempting a question from the Question and Answer section.

Key concepts

Key concepts are either defined or shown in bold. You should also have a business studies dictionary to hand.

Analysis

Under this heading there are suggestions on how topic areas could lend themselves to analysis. During your course and the revision period you should refer to these opportunities. Test and practise your understanding of the variety of ways in which a logical argument or line of reasoning can be developed.

Evaluation

Under this heading general opportunities for evaluation are highlighted within particular topic areas.

Integration

Under the heading, 'Links', the scope for linking different topic areas is shown. Most business problems have many dimensions and a student who can show, for example, the effect of a marketing problem on a company's finances or its personnel will be rewarded. Look for these opportunities to integrate. The introduction to both the Marketing and Finance sections of the AQA specification reads as follows: 'Candidates are expected to gain an understanding of marketing/accounting and finance in an integrated context within the organisation.'

Market analysis

The market and market segmentation

Market: a place where buyers and sellers meet.
A company must recognise which market it is in. Stagecoach, for example, sees itself as being in the travel industry, not as a 'bus company'. Try to identify the 'market' for some well-known companies. Compare your ideas with those of your friends.

Market size: this can be measured in two ways — the volume of sales (e.g. cars sold) or the value of sales (in pounds).
Remember that market size can increase through extra sales of goods, but also through persuading customers to pay higher prices. 'Trainers' are a good example of this idea.

Market growth: the percentage change in sales over a period of time.
Growth markets offer potential for increased sales but they also encourage competition. A company dominating a low growth market can 'milk' its 'cash cows' to boost its profits.

Market share: expressed as:

$$\text{Market share (\%)} = \frac{\text{sales of one product or brand (or company)}}{\text{total sales in the market}} \times 100$$

This is an excellent measure of success because it can only increase if a company is performing better than its rivals. In the case of Ford, its car sales in the UK increased in total in 2001 because of market growth, but its percentage share fell because sales of other car manufacturers (such as Citroën and Mercedes) increased more quickly.

> **Analysis** Analysis can take the form of:
> - identifying the implications of the market size for a small firm
> - investigating how market growth (or decline) will affect a new/small/large firm
> - examining the benefits of a high market share (or problems of a small market share)

Market segmentation: the strategy whereby an organisation divides a market into subsections (segments). These segments will react in different ways to different products or marketing approaches.

Types of segmentation
- age
- social class
- geographic
- frequency of purchase
- gender
- lifestyle
- usage
- residential

> **Analysis** Identify the segments that are important for the particular situation being studied. For example, age and gender tend to have a major influence on sales of many magazines, but geographical factors will be less important. Marketing strategies and the marketing mix must suit the targeted segments.

Reasons for segmentation

- to increase market share
- to extend products into new markets
- to assist new product development
- to diversify products and markets

Analysis Find examples of uses of market segmentation in order to increase market share, assist new product development etc.

Evaluation Successful segmentation requires market segments to be:
- identifiable
- distinct
- reachable

Gender, for example, is a useful method of segmentation because a person's sex is easy to identify, different sexes can be targeted through specific known media, and gender has a distinct impact on tastes for certain products. However, it does depend on the product. For products such as potatoes, it is hard to identify obvious segments, although 'lifestyle' is likely to be relevant.

Links The examples in the table below illustrate how marketing analysis links to other marketing concepts. This is not an exhaustive list, but suggests some possible links. Try to extend these by adding your own examples.

Tip: as the course progresses, try to identify links between these ideas and other activities such as 'Finance', 'People' and 'External Influences'.

Market analysis topic	Links to Marketing strategy	Links to Marketing planning
Market size	Small firms may need to use **niche marketing** to avoid direct competition. Large markets are crucial for **mass marketing,** and encourage **product differentiation.**	Large-scale **promotion** requires a large market. Retailers will be more willing to stock **(place)** products that have many buyers. In competitive markets, **price** is critical, but oligopolies use **promotion** more heavily.
Market growth	The **Boston matrix** links market growth and market share. The **product life cycle** of the generic product shows the scope for future growth.	Products with a **high income elasticity of demand** will grow as countries become richer. Skilled use of **promotion** can increase a market (e.g. replica football shirts).
Market share (%)	The **Boston matrix** links market share and market growth. **Niche markets** represent small percentage shares but can reap high sales incomes.	The company with the largest market share is likely to be a **price leader**. These **products** will gain esteem and can rely on word-of-mouth **promotion**. A decline in market share will encourage **extension strategies**.
Market segmentation	A market segment prepared to pay a premium price will help marketing to **add value**. **Differentiated marketing** relies on identifying market segments.	**Promotions** will be placed in media according to the segment that a company wishes to target. The **market price** will be higher if the product is targeted at high income groups or trendsetters/early adopters.

Market research

Market research is the systematic and objective **collection**, **analysis** and **evaluation** of information relating to markets and marketing.

Collection of information

Sources
There are two sources of information, **primary** and **secondary**.

Primary

Primary information is information collected first hand for a specific purpose. Primary comes second — it should only be used to fill the gaps.

Advantages:
- more relevant
- can show qualitative information (e.g. reasons why)

Disadvantages:
- expensive
- time-consuming

Secondary

Secondary information is information that has already been collected for a different purpose. Secondary information should be referred to first.

Advantages:
- already available
- cheaper

Disadvantages:
- possibly dated
- may be unreliable
- may be irrelevant

Content
Information can be **quantitative** or **qualitative**.

Quantitative

Quantitative information is based on numbers. It raises the following three questions:
- how many?
- who?
- how often?

It is excellent for analysis but it does not explain why people act in this way.

Qualitative

Qualitative information is based on subjective factors:
- why?
- how?

With this information, an organisation can plan appropriate strategies.

Sampling
Market research is undertaken by selecting a group of respondents whose views should be representative of the target market as a whole. This is called sampling. Two kinds of sampling are:

Random — each member of the population has an equal chance of being chosen.

Quota — this method splits the population into groups, each sharing a common feature (e.g. age, gender). The number of interviewees in each classification is fixed, to reflect their percentage with respect to total population.

Large samples increase reliability but cost more. Small samples decrease costs but are less reliable. A firm must balance the need to be accurate against the desire to limit costs. A sample size that is large enough to give 95% confidence in the results is a good size.

The **problems of sampling** are:
- unrepresentative samples (e.g. asking the wrong people)
- bias in answers or questions (e.g. questions that encourage lies)
- locating respondents (e.g. finding people who watch a particular television programme)

Analysis of information

Market research analysis involves the study of data in order to draw conclusions or provide advice. When considering the outcome of market research you should take into account the points below.

Trends or directions of change in the data
- It is safe to project that trends will continue into the future. You can, however, argue that a trend will not continue (e.g. if a market is reaching saturation). Mobile phones sales are a good example of maket saturation.
- If there is no clear direction of change, is there an obvious cycle? The figures shown may be seasonal. Does the product being discussed support this logic?

Links between different sets of data
- If two sets of data follow the same trend, is one causing the other to change? Increased advertising, for example, should lead to more sales.
- This link might be inverse (negative). Price increases will lead to lower sales.
- If there are no links when logically there could be (e.g. sales not rising during an advertising campaign or following a price cut), you can judge (evaluate) that the change is not having the expected effect.

Comparisons
- An increase in Product X may look impressive, but is it a success if all the other companies are growing faster? Similarly, a decline may show a company that is reasonably efficient if its rivals are declining more noticeably.
- Certain data are always useful for comparison, e.g. inflation and growth rates.

Other factors
- There is scope to use your imagination here. A useful approach is to look at the other departments in a business — how would they be affected by the data?
- Look at the company's objectives. Will they be affected? Should they be modified?
- External influences — what is the state of the market/the economy? Is the government influencing the company's position? Are its competitors changing their marketing?

Additional information

- Put yourself in the position of the person or company in the case. Useful information could be internal (e.g. changes in price or advertising) or external (e.g. changes in laws or bad publicity).

Evaluation of information

Evaluation of market research involves asking the following questions:

- How reliable are the data?
- What internal factors might influence the situation — the effect on personnel, production, and other departments?
- What external factors might influence the situation — economic changes, changes in fashion or taste, etc?
- Are there sufficient quantitative and qualitative data?
- What other information is needed?
- Is there sufficient time to research? Fast-moving industries may limit market research in order to avoid delaying the release of a new product or marketing campaign.

According to Anita Roddick (The Body Shop): 'Market research is like looking in the rear view mirror — it tells me where I have been rather than where I am going.'

Conclusion

The relative value of market research depends on the following:

- Cost — this needs to be kept to a minimum, without jeopardising its accuracy.
- Reliability — the research needs to be as up to date as possible, and without any bias.
- Relevance — primary research should provide the answers that you need.
- Pace of change — market research is less valuable if the market and tastes are constantly changing.

  Links Market research underpins all of marketing and therefore influences all other marketing activities. It also dictates the products that will be developed and marketing techniques used, thus relating closely to activities such as operations management, personnel and production.

Marketing objectives and strategy

The following definitions are useful in this topic.

Marketing objectives: the goals of the marketing function within an organisation.

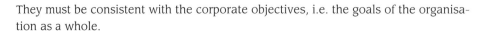

They must be consistent with the corporate objectives, i.e. the goals of the organisation as a whole.

Marketing strategies: long-term or medium-term plans, devised at senior management level, and designed to achieve the marketing objectives.

Marketing tactics: short-term marketing measures adopted in order to meet the needs of a short-term threat or opportunity. Ideally, they will be consistent with the marketing objectives and strategies, but this may not always be the case.

Marketing objectives

The objectives can be categorised as follows:
A   Size — increase sales or market share.
B   Market positioning, e.g. appeal to a particular segment.
C   Innovation/increase in product range.
D   Creation of brand loyalty/goodwill.
E   Security/survival.
F   Reach new market segments.

Marketing strategies

The marketing objectives above influence the marketing strategies. Each of the four strategies outlined below relates more closely to some objectives than others.

(1) Niche or mass marketing: should the firm aim its product at a particular market segment (niche marketing) or a mass market, appealing to the whole market? Both niche and mass marketing strategies can meet most of the marketing objectives. On the one hand, sales can be increased by attracting a mass market, and this will provide security too. On the other, the right niche ensures market positioning, and innovative products will reach new segments.

(2) Product life cycle: the firm should aim to have as many products in 'maturity' as possible. To achieve this in the long run the firm needs to have a policy of new product development, so that it has products in the introduction and growth stages. This strategy helps to achieve objectives A, C and E (and possibly F).

(3) Product portfolio analysis: the aim here is to create a balance of products with widespread appeal. The Boston matrix is the usual way of showing this strategy. Firms aim to produce products with a high market share (cash cows if market growth is low, stars if the market is growing quickly). They need to think carefully about retaining products with a low market share (dogs or problem children). Dogs, however, shouldn't be written off too lightly. Cadbury's Whole Nut, for example, which could be seen to be a dog, has a 1% share of a low growth market (confectionery) but this represents almost £40 million of sales per year. Careful analysis can help a firm to attain objectives A, B, C and E. 'Gap analysis' can be used to investigate a product range to see if there are any market segments to which the product does not appeal; new products can be tailored to fit any gap that has been discovered.

(4) Adding value: marketing can add value by creating a unique selling point (USP). If a firm can improve customer awareness and goodwill through making its product different from rival products, it can increase both its sales volume and price. Loyal customers are also less likely to stop buying the firm's product. This strategy can meet all six of the marketing objectives. *See if you can work out how all six objectives can be reached through adding value by creating a USP.*

Analysis Analysis can take the form of:
- linking the strategies to objectives, showing how they influence each other
- linking strategies and objectives to market research data
- comparing the relative merits of different strategies
- showing how chosen strategies will lead to different marketing mixes
- indicating how a specific strategy will affect the business
- studying the consequences of a strategy
- analysing the similarities and differences between the strategies — whether they complement or conflict with each other

More specifically analysis might focus on:
- the implications of the different stages of the product life cycle
- the consequences of a short (or long) product life cycle
- showing the benefits to a firm of a particular USP
- examining the implications of operating in a niche market
- comparing the merits of different extension strategies

Evaluation The integrated nature of any marketing decision lends itself to evaluation. A fruitful area for both analysis and evaluation is a study of the constraints that influence marketing objectives and strategies.

Internal constraints
- Research and development — does the company have the skills and technology to release new products?
- Finances — will marketing campaigns damage cash flow; are sources of finance available for research and development?
- Reputation — new products can appeal to new customers and improve a firm's reputation for innovation, but a badly researched product can damage a firm's image.
- Production and operations — is the production department capable of manufacturing a new product; will retailers stock it; will distribution systems need to be modified? The costs of these changes should be considered.
- Other products — will the new product cannibalise (take sales from) existing company products?

External constraints
- Consumer tastes — are these known, predictable and stable, and does the product suit consumers' needs?
- The economy — is there growth in the economy, and if so, will this benefit the product? Will the government's economic policy affect the firm, i.e. through changes in taxes and interest rates?

- Competition — how will competitors react to any changes in a firm's marketing? Will this limit the success of any strategy?
- Suppliers — can they provide the organisation with the necessary materials?

Marketing planning

The marketing mix

The main variables that make up a company's marketing strategy are **the four Ps** — product, price, promotion and place.

Product

Product is the central feature of the marketing mix. The key elements to be understood are:

- **Design of a product** — to the consumer this means reliability, safety, convenience of use, and whether it is fashionable, aesthetic and durable. To the firm, the key elements are whether the product satisfies consumer tastes, the financial viability, its effect on reputation, and whether the company can produce it without difficulty.
- **New product development** — you need to know the stages involved in introducing a new product (from initial screening to the final launch). Link new product development to the product life cycle, Boston matrix, brainstorming, market research and R&D (research and development). These will be the sources of new product ideas.

Price

The factors that influence price are based on the forces of demand and supply. Factors influencing demand are the nature of the product, consumers' incomes, competitors' products, tastes and fashion. Supply is affected by costs of inputs (raw materials and wages mainly), technology, production methods and environmental conditions. The type of market is crucial too — the number of competitors will influence a firm's pricing, and its power to set prices will depend on its market share.

You need to know the difference between **pricing methods**, **strategies** and **tactics**. There are overlaps between these classifications but a simple distinction is outlined below.

Pricing methods

Pricing methods are used to calculate the actual price to be set. Such methods include:

- **Cost-plus pricing:** the price set is the average cost plus a sum to ensure a profit.
- **Contribution pricing:** the price is set to cover variable costs, and contribute to fixed costs/profit.

- **Price discrimination:** a higher price is charged to some customers who will pay such a price.

Pricing strategies

Pricing strategies are adopted over the medium to long term to achieve marketing objectives. Such strategies include:

- **Skimming pricing:** a high price is set to yield a high profit margin.
- **Penetration pricing:** low prices are set to break into a market.
- **Price leader:** a large company that sets a market price that price takers (smaller firms) follow.
- **Predator (or destroyer) pricing:** very low prices are set to drive other firms out of the market.

Pricing tactics

Pricing tactics are adopted in the short term to suit particular situations.

- **Loss leaders:** very low prices are used to encourage consumers to buy other, fully priced, products.
- **Psychological pricing:** prices are set to give an impression of value (e.g. £99 rather than £100).

Promotion

Promotion attempts to draw the consumers' attention to the product, brand or company. It can be **above-the-line** or **below-the-line**.

- **Above-the-line:** this is advertising through media — newspapers, television, radio, the cinema and posters.
- **Below-the-line:** this refers to all other promotion such as public relations, merchandising, sponsorship, direct marketing, personal selling and competitions.

Advertising can be **informative** or **persuasive**. It aims to raise awareness, publicise changes and new products, and increase brand loyalty. **Promotions** (except public relations and sponsorship) tend to be more targeted, trying to clinch the final purchase through special offers, persuasive selling or point-of-sale displays. Companies tend to plan advertising and promotions that support each other (e.g. *Reader's Digest* advertising that its subscribers will receive a direct mail offer).

Place

This involves getting products to the places where customers can buy them. Shops do not automatically give space to suppliers. Many salespeople are employed to persuade retailers to stock their product rather than trying to persuade customers to buy it.

Traditionally the method of getting a product from the producer to the customer was producer ⇒ wholesaler ⇒ retailer ⇒ consumer. Many companies now bypass the wholesaler.

Think of companies/products that bypass the wholesaler. Do any bypass the retailer? Study how the internet is affecting distribution.

Factors influencing the method of distribution include:

- type of product (e.g. perishable)
- geography of the market (is it scattered?)
- complexity of the product (may need direct contact with producer or an expert retailer)

Analysis This is an area ripe for analysis, although it is not always fruitful. Questions will require you to apply the marketing mix, and the wording of the question may require specific application (e.g. asking for a plan or method to increase sales of a set product). Be aware that the four Ps are not equally important in all cases.

Product: this is central. If it does not satisfy the customers, then the other elements cannot really overcome this. However, effective use of the other three Ps can assist success.

Price: low prices can increase sales but this will reduce the profit margin and the firm may not be able to meet demand, a good example being Kit-Kat Chunky. Look at the circumstances in which different pricing methods or strategies can be used (e.g. when should a firm use price skimming?).

Promotion: what is the most appropriate method for your product and market, and will it be cost effective?

Place: do you want to keep more control of the process? Will distributors demand too much profit and will retailers stock your product?

Evaluation In bold print below are two example questions. In order to evaluate, the important skill is to put yourself into the position of the firm in the question and ask: 'What decision would I take and why?'

What is the most appropriate marketing mix in a particular situation?

Product: if a particular function is required (e.g. lighting), the product becomes more crucial than one that is bought for image purposes only. What is the product? People go to a sporting event that they can watch on television — they are prepared to pay more for the 'augmented' product.

Price: this is particularly important for products which appeal to people on low incomes. What is the price elasticity of demand?

Promotion: items sold to lifestyle groups on the basis of their image rely heavily on promotion. Goods with high income elasticity can be promoted in magazines read by a particular market segment.

Place: impulse buys need to be readily available and so place is vital (a minority of chocolate purchases are planned beforehand).

How much control does the company have over its marketing mix?

Product: you must react to competition, expectations of customers, and government legislation. People are naturally conservative and so opportunities may be less inviting than they seem at first.

Price: unless you are a monopoly you will be limited in your scope to change price. In oligopoly (competition with a few firms) businesses try to avoid price competition.

Promotion: your customers must be attracted to your promotions and so you will need to understand their tastes. In oligopoly, businesses use promotion as their main method of competition.

Place: you must use methods that customers will accept. In practice, this decision is often taken by the retailer rather than the producer — it depends on the bargaining power of the two sides.

Elasticity of demand

Types of elasticity

Elasticity of demand measures the responsiveness of a change in the quantity demanded of a good or service to a change in the value of another variable.

The two main formulae for business studies students are:

$$\textbf{price elasticity of demand} = \frac{\% \text{ change in quantity demanded}}{\% \text{ change in } \textbf{price}}$$

$$\textbf{income elasticity of demand} = \frac{\% \text{ change in quantity demanded}}{\% \text{ change in } \textbf{income}}$$

Note: be wary of using raw data to calculate elasticities, especially in coursework, as the changes in demand will also have been influenced by other factors. It is impossible to isolate changes in price from other factors that influence demand.

Price elasticity of demand

Elastic demand: if the change in price leads to a greater percentage change in the quantity demanded (ignoring the minus sign), then the calculation will yield an answer greater than 1.

Inelastic demand: if the change in price leads to a smaller percentage change in the quantity demanded, then the calculation will yield an answer less than 1.

The factors influencing the price elasticity of demand are:
- necessity
- habit
- availability of substitutes
- income of consumers
- brand loyalty

Income elasticity of demand

Income elasticity of demand indicates how demand will be affected by changes in income. As a general rule, a 10% increase in income will lead to approximately a 10% increase in demand for products.
- For the **average product** the income elasticity of demand will therefore be 1.
- For **luxury products** the answer will be greater than 1. Expenditure on holidays, for example, tends to increase by a larger percentage as an economy grows richer.

- For **necessities** there is likely to be a rise in demand that is smaller than the rise in income. This will give an elasticity that is greater than zero, but less than 1.
- For some products, such as tripe, demand has fallen as people have experienced increases in income and can afford better alternatives. These products have a negative income elasticity of demand and are known as **inferior goods**.

Analysis Elasticity of demand can be used to interpret the market. A brief table of data, such as the one below, can provide a lot of information.

	Product A	Product B
Price elasticity of demand	−3.5	−0.5
Income elasticity of demand	+0.6	+2.0

Conclusions for Product A

Price elasticity of demand is −3.5 (very elastic). A change in price leads to a larger change in quantity. This product is not a necessity and appears to have many close substitutes.

Income elasticity of demand is +0.6 (low). As incomes increase, this product will gain sales but will not keep pace with most products. It is probably a product that does not appeal to richer consumers.

Conclusions for Product B

Price elasticity of demand is −0.5 (inelastic). The product is a necessity or has no close substitutes.

Income elasticity of demand is +2.0 (high). This product is a luxury, showing a large percentage increase in sales as income rises. This would suggest that the price elasticity is inelastic because it has no close substitutes or is habit-forming, rather than being a necessity.

Marketing strategies for Product A

Short-term
- Charge a lower price to increase sales revenue, but not if the company is operating on low profit margins.
- Change the image — as the economy grows the sales of this product will grow at a slower rate and so market share will be lost. However, during a recession the decline in sales would be relatively small.

Long-term
- Reposition the product in order to appeal to higher income sectors.
- Alternatively, if profit margins are reasonable, the company may keep the product unchanged. It may act as a cash cow, and in periods of fierce competition price cuts should enable the company to generate high sales volumes.

Marketing strategies for Product B

Short-term
- increase price
- aim for high 'value added'

Long-term
- this product appears to be a cash cow, and should be 'milked'
- keep the price high
- safeguard the product's image

Evaluation   In order to evaluate you could:
- recommend an analysis of other factors/changes that influence demand
- point out that elasticities do not stay the same: views of products and markets can change in the short and long term
- look beyond the marketing implications
- make it clear that recommended policies must be consistent with corporate and marketing objectives
- ask whether the organisation could finance the suggested strategies

Classification of costs, profit, contribution and breakeven analysis

Classification of costs

Costs can be classified in relation to **output and time** or **product**.

Output and time

The costs relating to output and time are **fixed costs** and **variable costs**.

Fixed costs are costs that do not vary directly with output in the short run (e.g. rent, stationery and salaries of administrative staff). **Variable costs** are costs that vary directly with output in the short run (e.g. raw materials and wages of operatives).

Total costs for a firm can be calculated by adding fixed costs and variable costs.

Companies use output and time to calculate the financial repercussions of changing the level of output. Businesses define two main time periods:
(1) The long-run — the time in which the scale of the firm can be changed (e.g. opening a new factory).
(2) The short-run — the period in which the scale cannot be changed (existing capacity must be used). Extra output is possible if there is spare capacity.

Product

The costs relating to product are **direct costs** and **indirect cost/overheads**.

Direct costs are those costs that can be related directly to a product or service (e.g. raw materials).

Indirect costs/overheads are those costs that cannot be related directly to a product or service (e.g. the managing director's salary).

Total costs for a product can be calculated by adding direct costs plus a percentage of the firm's indirect costs (overheads). For a firm making only one product you would need to add all (100%) of the indirect costs.

This classification enables a firm to allocate costs to individual products and so measure their efficiency.

Profit

Revenue (or **sales revenue**) is the value of sales over a given time (usually 1 year). It is also known as **turnover**, **sales turnover** or **income**.

Revenue = volume (quantity) of goods sold × selling price of each good

Profit is calculated by subtracting total costs from revenue.

Profit = revenue – total costs

Contribution

Contribution per unit shows how much the sale of one product will go towards (contribute to) meeting the fixed costs of a company. Once fixed costs have been met, sales of the product contribute to profit. This concept is useful in calculating break-even.

Contribution per unit = selling price – direct cost per unit

The total 'contribution' of a product can be calculated in two ways:

Either the contribution per unit × number of units sold
or   total sales revenue – total direct costs

Analysis Calculations involving costs and revenue primarily test **application** skills. Analysis can be shown in a number of ways:
- revenue and costs — analysis of simple profit calculations, showing reasons for the results
- revenue and costs — analysis of simple profit calculations, showing the implications (effects) of the results
- advice on how to improve profit, or to assess how a particular change might influence the figures
- commentary on other, non-financial factors that should be studied before drawing conclusions from the data

Evaluation These calculations will normally identify clear situations, and so there is little scope for evaluation (judgement). However, possibilities for evaluation include:
- revenue and costs — advice based on simple profit calculations, but allowing for changes in circumstances that will modify the figures
- revenue and costs — advice based on simple profit calculations, but needing to take into account non-financial factors such as the company's image
- judging the significance of the level of, or relative balance between, fixed and variable costs
- evaluating the use of these figures in (static) break-even analysis
- judging why one firm's costs vary from those of another, and the implications of this (see Question 4 on p. 56 for an example)
- questioning whether the profit is of high quality (sustainable)
- asking how this year's actual revenue, costs and profit compare to forecasts, previous figures and rival firms' records

An underpinning theme in AS is that 'business behaviour can be studied from the perspectives of a range of stakeholders including customers, managers, …employees'. It is therefore possible (but unlikely) that a judgement will be required from the view of one of these stakeholders.

Simple breakeven analysis

Breakeven analysis investigates the minimum output and sales that a company requires in order for its revenue to cover its costs. At a zero level of output, the company will have incurred fixed costs (buildings and machinery) without making any revenue from sales. It will therefore make a loss.

For each item that the company produces, its revenue will equal the price of the item, but it will incur more costs (direct costs, such as raw materials).

Price per unit – direct cost per unit measures the contribution per unit. This shows the amount of money that each unit provides (contributes) towards paying off the fixed costs (or creating a profit, once the fixed costs have been met). So, a product with a selling price of £8 and direct costs of £6 will contribute £2 per unit (£8 – £6), whilst one with a price of £7 and direct costs of £3 will contribute £4 per unit.

The **total contribution** is the contribution per unit multiplied by the number of units. In the example above, 200 units would provide a contribution of £800 (£4 × 200) towards fixed costs and profit.

Breakeven analysis makes the following **assumptions**:
- The selling price remains the same, regardless of the number of units sold.
- Fixed costs remain the same, regardless of the number of units of output.
- Variable costs vary in direct proportion to output.

Calculating the breakeven output

$$\text{Breakeven output} = \frac{\text{fixed cost (£)}}{\text{contribution per unit (£)}}$$

A product with a price of £9 and direct costs of £4 will contribute £5 for every unit sold. At £5 per unit the company would need to sell 400 units in order to pay fixed costs of £2,000, and so break even.

$$\text{Breakeven output} = \frac{£2,000}{£9 - £4 = £5} = 400 \text{ units}$$

Plotting breakeven on a graph

Sales revenue can be plotted against units sold. At a higher price, the gradient of the line will be steeper than at a low price. The figure below shows the sales revenue at different levels of output for a product with a selling price of £8 per unit.

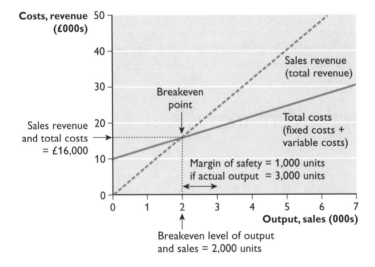

In order to produce goods or services, a company must purchase fixed assets. These **fixed costs** must be paid, regardless of the actual units of output. In the figure, the fixed costs are £10,000, and will be £10,000 whether output is zero or 5,000 units.

Variable costs will vary directly with output. At zero output no variable costs will be incurred. Each unit produced will require additional inputs of variable factors (primarily raw materials and direct labour). A company might find that raw materials cost £2 per unit and wages are £1 per unit. Variable costs are therefore £3 per unit.

By adding fixed costs and variable costs we can calculate the **total costs** of production at different levels of output.

It can be seen that costs are incurred even if no units are sold (because fixed costs are paid in anticipation that units will be sold). Low levels of sales are therefore unlikely to produce a profit. As sales (and output) increase, the fixed costs become less of a burden as the fixed cost per unit (the average fixed cost) falls. For example, if output is 100 units, the £10,000 fixed costs equal £100 per unit (£10,000/100). If output rises to 2,000 units, the £10,000 fixed costs equal only £5 per unit (£10,000/2000). Consequently, firms benefit from high levels of output and sales.

In the figure, the **breakeven point** is indicated by an arrow. The output required to break even is 2,000 units, at which level the sales revenue and costs are £16,000.

The **margin of safety** is the difference between the actual output and the breakeven output. If actual output is 3,000 units, then the margin of safety is 1,000 units (3,000 − 2,000).

Analysis   Breakeven analysis (despite the name) deals mainly with application skills. Scope for analysis can involve the uses and advantages or disadvantages of breakeven.

Uses and advantages of breakeven analysis

(1) The main benefit of a breakeven chart is that it can show the different levels of profit arising from the various levels of output and sales that might be achieved.

(2) Breakeven can be adapted to discover at which point a company can reach a particular profit level (a more realistic aim for most companies). This identifies the contribution needed to pay both the fixed costs and the target profit figure. For example, suppose the target profit is £10,000, fixed costs are £20,000 and the contribution per unit is £5. To break even the required output is £20,000/£5 = 4,000 units. To make £10,000, the required output is (£20,000 + £10,000)/£5 = 6,000 units.

(3) A new firm can see from the breakeven point how long it will take before it can make a profit and so assess whether the business is viable.

(4) Breakeven charts are quick and easy to complete, saving time for a business.

(5) Breakeven calculations and graphs allow a company to conduct 'what if?' analysis, investigating the impact on breakeven and profit of changes in:

- the selling price
- the variable cost per unit
- the fixed costs

(Note: point 5, relating to changes in the variables in a breakeven chart, is in the A2 part of the A-level and should not be tested on an AS paper.)

Disadvantages of breakeven analysis

(1) Information may be unreliable.

(2) Sales and output are unlikely to be exactly the same.

(3) The analysis is static — a new diagram or calculation is needed every time there is a change.

(4) The ideas of non-changing fixed costs and constant selling price and variable costs per unit are all questionable.

Evaluation   Possible opportunities for evaluation include:

- evaluating the usefulness of breakeven analysis
- passing judgement on the relative strengths of the advantages and disadvantages in a particular case

- using a breakeven chart to weigh up the desirability of an action, along with other information
- in A2, changes to values and their relative impact could be evaluated

Company accounts

Cash-flow management

Cash-flow management involves careful control of cash in the short term in order to ensure **liquidity** (the ability of a firm to meet its short-term debts). A business sustaining losses will fail, but even a profitable firm can fold if it is unable to pay a creditor who requires payment in cash.

The cash-flow forecast

Too much cash means a firm will have less machinery and stock than it can afford and so makes less profit. Too little cash will threaten survival if a bill cannot be paid. In order to maintain the right balance, a firm plans its cash holdings by compiling a cash-flow forecast. This enables an organisation to identify potential problems, and take appropriate action (e.g. arranging a bank overdraft).

> **Analysis** You should be aware of the factors that can cause inaccurate cash-flow projections and/or the consequences of poor forecasting. However, analysis should focus on the **management** of cash flow or the **causes** of or **solutions** to cash-flow problems.

Managing cash flow

Cash flow can be improved by the following methods:

- **Debtors** are customers who owe a business money. If a company decides to give customers credit (to help sales), it must control its debtors to ensure prompt payment.
- A company may choose to **factor** its debts. This means that a factoring company will give immediate payment of cash to the company and then collect the debts for itself (but it will charge for its service).
- **Managing stock** — low stock levels reduce storage space, and the chances of damage, deterioration and obsolescence. High stock levels allow companies to benefit from bulk-buying discounts and minimise the risk of lost sales and goodwill through a failure to meet customer needs. A company has to weigh up the relative merits of both options.
- **Sale and leaseback** — a company that owns fixed assets can sell these for an immediate lump sum of cash and then lease (rent) them back. However, in the long run, the rental payments are likely to exceed the lump sum received.

Causes of cash-flow problems

The main causes of cash-flow problems are:

- **Over-investment** in fixed assets leaving no money to pay bills.
- **Overtrading** — producing too many goods and running out of cash.
- **Credit sales** — increasing sales and thus expenses, but with no cash received until a later date.
- **Stockpiling** — tying up assets in stock.
- **Seasonal factors** — low sales revenue or high costs during part of the year.
- **Changing tastes** — products do not sell.
- **Management errors** — poor market research or budgetary control leading to cash shortages.

Solutions to cash-flow problems

The main solutions can be matched to the initial causes.

- **Over-investment** — sale and leaseback can be used to raise a lump sum of cash in the short term.
- **Overtrading** — better market research should eliminate mistaken confidence that causes this problem.
- **Credit sales** — careful scrutiny of repayments ensures that the customers (the debtors) pay promptly.
- **Stockpiling** — more efficient stock control minimises waste and stock levels, and therefore costs.
- **Seasonal factors** — diversify so that products sell throughout the year (e.g. Mars making ice cream).
- **Changing tastes** — market research helps to anticipate changes. A contingency fund should be set aside.
- **Management errors** — improved planning and control reduces the risk of errors.

Evaluation   Based on the above analysis you could evaluate:

- the best way of managing cash flow
- the most likely causes of cash-flow problems
- the optimum solutions for cash-flow problems
- the interrelationships between the above three factors
- conclusions that could be drawn from the data
- discussions based on the reliability of the information

Sources of finance

Finance has to be used to fund two types of expenditure:

Capital expenditure — this is spending on items that can be used time and time again (fixed assets). It may take a long time before these items generate enough revenue to pay for themselves, so a long-term source of finance is ideal.

Revenue expenditure — this is spending on current, day-to-day costs such as the purchase of raw materials and payment of wages. Such expenditure provides a quick return, so the company should rely on a short- or medium-term source of finance.

Sources may be **internal** (generated by the firm itself) or **external** (provided by outsiders).

Internal sources

As there is no requirement to pay an external agent for the use of these funds they can generally be used for any length of time:

- long term (more than 5 years)
- medium term (1 to 5 years)
- short term (less than 1 year)

Internal sources of finance include:

(1) Retained (trading) profit — shareholders expect a share of the profit as a dividend, but the remaining profit can be retained and used. This is a cheap and flexible form of finance, but managers should recognise that its main cost is the opportunity cost (the next best alternative foregone) and that it should be retained for a specific purpose.

(2) Sale of assets — selling fixed assets can allow a business to develop more profitable ventures. A firm in difficulties may sell fixed assets in order to survive a crisis, but in the long term this is likely to lower its profitability.

(3) Working capital — short-term needs can be met from the current assets (as long as current liabilities are not too high).

External sources

(1) Ordinary shares — these are known as risk capital. Holders receive their dividends after the preference shareholders and there is no guaranteed percentage dividend. In profitable years a very high dividend may be paid, but an unsuccessful company may pay no dividend to its ordinary shareholders. These shares appeal to investors prepared to face an element of risk in return for (usually) higher rewards.

(2) Venture capital — this is provided in the form of loans or the acquisition of share capital. Venture capitalists usually invest in small/medium high-risk companies that might also produce an excellent return.

(3) Loan capital — providers of loan capital are known as creditors. They charge interest on the loan and must be paid before any dividends are received by share-holders. Similarly, if a business liquidates (closes down), the money raised from the sale of its assets must be paid in full to creditors before any payment is made to the shareholders. Three kinds of loan capital are outlined below.

(a) Debentures — these are long-term loans made to a business at an agreed fixed percentage rate of interest repayable on a stated date. Twenty-five year debentures were common, but the pace of change and higher interest rates have meant that they are generally issued for shorter time periods.

(b) Bank loans — these are provided for a specific, agreed purpose. The business in question will be required to provide a form of security, and will repay the loan and interest on a regular basis over an agreed period of time.

(c) Bank overdraft — this is when a bank allows a firm to overspend its current account in the bank up to an agreed overdraft limit and for a stated time period. Overdrafts are widely used and flexible, and can overcome the cash-flow problems suffered by businesses whose sales are seasonal or which need to buy materials in advance of a large order. The rate of interest is variable and only charged daily on the amount by which the account is overdrawn. Technically, the bank can demand immediate repayment. In practice, overdraft agreements are often renewed and are treated as a reliable source of finance.

Analysis The firm will make decisions on the sources of finance, but what will it consider?

- The length of repayment is always critical. Short-term needs must not be financed in a way that commits the business to expenditure a long time into the future. Similarly, **short-term sources will put pressure on a firm's cash flow if the expenditure only brings in profit in the distant future**.
- The availability of finance is an issue. Can the company attract shareholders? **Will it be able to provide security for a bank loan?**
- Ownership of the firm. Selling ordinary shares means that buyers will own part of the company. This will spread the risks but it will dilute control. **Will the founders/directors still be elected to run the company if they no longer own most of the shares?**
- External factors. High interest rates will make loans less attractive, **especially a long-run fixed interest charge such as a debenture**.
- Future forecasts. Will these be good enough to attract investors or persuade the bank manager? Does the company have a good reputation for accurate forecasts?
- The use of the finance. Will it generate profit? A firm should only raise finance if the return exceeds the cost of repaying the finance.
- The opportunity cost. Is there a more attractive use of the money?
- The risk level. Ordinary shares are known as risk capital and should be used to finance risky projects — **the company can pay no dividend if there are problems**.
- Shareholders' reactions. Will they support it? If they disagree and sell shares, the price of the shares will fall **and make that form of finance more difficult in the future**.
- Liquidity. Will cash flow be affected? This is a particular risk if working capital is being used.
- Sale of assets. This can be a double benefit — receiving a lump sum and getting rid of a loss-making part of the business. But have you avoided the issue — **could it have been turned into a profit-making element of the business? You are likely to receive less money if an asset is seen to be creating losses for your company.**
- Reputation. Sale of assets or an overdraft may be seen to be a sign of weakness — the former almost certainly is.

Evaluation This is an area of Module 1 that lends itself to evaluation based on information provided. All of the above analytical points can lead on to evaluation. Judging the suitability of sources of finance in a given situation will test evaluative skills. The points under the 'analysis' section in **bold** are illustrations of judgement (evaluation) taking place.

Links A basic requirement of the AS/A-level course is to investigate the integrated nature of business. The examples in the table below illustrate how 'company accounts' links to other accounting and finance concepts. Extend these links by adding your own examples and repeating the exercise for the other elements (Costs, revenue and profit, and Budgeting). As the course progresses, try to identify links between these ideas and other activities such as 'Finance', 'People' and 'External Influences'. There are also close links between cash flow and sources of finance.

Short-term sources of finance are mainly used to overcome potential cash-flow problems in the short term. An organisation projecting a cash-flow problem will need to plan a suitable source of finance if the projection cannot be changed.

Accounting and Finance topic	Links to Costs, revenue, profit and breakeven	Links to Budgeting
Cash-flow forecasting — purpose, construction and perils	Constructing a cash-flow forecast requires information on **costs and revenue**. This helps a firm to identify potential profits and losses. If a firm knows its output and sales, it can calculate the **breakeven point** and **margin of safety**.	Budgets are based on **cash-flow forecasts**, and vice versa. Once probable costs have been calculated, the appropriate budget will be allocated. If the cash-flow forecast runs into problems, then it is probable that the budget allocation is wrong.
Improving cash flow	All of the main ways of improving cash flow rely on efficient handling of costs and revenue. **Factoring** means an organisation receives cash from its sales more quickly. The same applies to **creditor control**. **Sale and leaseback** means a steady regular payment in return for a one-off boost. Efficient **stock control** reduces some costs.	Careful budgeting spreads expenditure and so improves cash flow. Monitoring of budget variances allows a company to foresee potential cash-flow problems. **Profit centres and cost centres** should improve efficiency and save costs, so improving cash flow.
Sources of finance	**Profit (retained)** is a major source of finance. **Fixed costs** usually require long-term financing so a business needs to know what these costs entail to plan its **bank loans, debentures** and other sources.	**Budgets** show how much money a business needs, so the amount it needs to borrow can be calculated. **Variances** show whether more short-term finance is needed to overcome a temporary problem.

Long-term sources of finance are used to overcome potential cash-flow problems too. If a company does not identify a source for its major expenditure on fixed assets, then it will experience cash-flow problems.

Budgeting, cost centres and profit centres

A budget is an agreed plan establishing in numerical or financial terms the policy to be pursued and the anticipated outcomes of that policy. Budgets are usually stated in terms of financial targets, relating to money allocated to support the organisation of a particular function, but they also include targets for revenue and output or sales volume.

The aims of budgeting

A budget may be set for the following reasons:

(1) To establish priorities by indicating the level of importance attached to a particular policy or division.

(2) To provide direction and coordination by ensuring that spending is geared towards the firm's aims.

(3) To assign responsibility by identifying the person who is directly responsible for any success or failure.

(4) To motivate staff by giving them greater responsibility and recognition when they meet targets.

(5) To improve efficiency by investigating reasons for failure and success.

(6) To encourage forward planning by studying possible outcomes.

Problems of budgeting

If the budgeting system is too rigid, certain undesirable consequences may occur:

- **Incorrect allocations.** A budget that is too generous may encourage inefficiency. A budget that is insufficient will demotivate staff and hinder progress through a lack of money.
- **External factors.** Changes outside the budget holders' control may affect their ability to stick to the plan.
- **Poor communication.** Budgets must be agreed between people who understand the area in question and also other, external factors.

The above problems can be overcome by **flexible budgeting** which allows amendments in response to changes. However, more flexible systems reduce the effectiveness of budgets as a means of control, and can lead to inefficiencies if close scrutiny is lost. Some firms adopt **zero budgeting**. This requires managers to justify any money allocated in order to ensure that allocations are not excessive.

Budgetary control

Budgetary control is the establishment of budgets and the continuous comparison of actual and budgeted results in order to ascertain variances from the plan and to provide a basis for revision of the objective or strategy.

Cost centres and profit centres

Budgetary responsibilities are carried out by **cost centres** and **profit centres**.
- **Cost centres** must ensure that the costs of an activity remain within a set budget, e.g. the purchasing department.
- **Profit centres** are required to generate both revenue and control costs, e.g. a branch of a supermarket.

Variance analysis

A variance represents the difference between the planned standard and the actual performance. If the variance represents a poorer performance than planned, it is known as an **adverse** or **unfavourable variance**, e.g. higher costs or lower sales revenue. If the variance represents a better performance than planned, it is known as a **favourable variance**, e.g. lower costs or higher sales revenue.

Identification of the cause of a variance can allow a company to:
- identify the responsibility
- take appropriate action

For an adverse variable the firm can investigate alternative methods if the factor is under its control. Favourable variances can be used to identify efficient methods that can be adopted more widely in the company.

Causes of variances
Variances in costs can be caused by changes in:
- storage and wastage of material
- material costs (cheaper or dearer)
- efficiency changes
- morale and efficiency of staff
- wages
- quality of material

Interpretation of variances
The following table shows how variances can be interpreted as being either favourable or adverse. In the variance column, (F) indicates a favourable variance and (A) an adverse variance.

Identity of budget	Planned	Actual	Variance
Cost of sales			
Materials	10,000	12,000	2,000 (A)
Wages	15,000	14,000	1,000 (F)
Overheads			
Admin. staff	4,000	8,000	4,000 (A)
Rent and rates	5,000	7,000	2,000 (A)
Marketing	6,000	1,000	5,000 (F)
Other costs	5,000	5,000	Nil
Total costs	45,000	47,000	2,000 (A)

Analysis Account for the variances to the planned budgets shown in the budget table above, indicating apparent areas of efficiency and inefficiency. Use the list of six factors to identify possible causes.

Tip: variances may be caused by the firm (internally) or external factors. It is often easier to identify external changes (e.g. high inflation, shortages of materials) than internal ones.

Note: variances caused by changes in the amount sold or the price charged are not in the specification for AS (although you can use them as ideas if you wish).

Analysis may also take the form of showing the:
- implications of budget variances
- benefits of budgeting to the firm
- difficulties and problems of budgeting

Evaluation Possible approaches to evaluation in this area of the specification are to:
- identify the key causes of variances
- assess the best solutions to adverse variances
- judge the usefulness of budgeting, the difficulties of projecting, and so on
- evaluate the pros and/or cons of profit centres and cost centres
- discuss the feasibility of solving problems

Budgets imply control — you could focus on the style of manager who would support these processes.

Note: a major limitation of budgets is the timing. Budgets are set before the event and so people are guessing what will happen in the future. Variances are assessed after the event, by which time the problems have passed.

Questions
&
Answers

In this section of the guide there are eight questions, each followed by two sample answers interspersed by examiner comments.

Questions

The questions are based on the format of the AS papers. The usual pattern is for the first parts of the questions to test knowledge, building into those that allow under-standing to be applied (application). The higher mark questions follow, with analysis (in which the reasoning is developed further) and evaluation (the making of a reasoned judgement).

This is not always the case. If a definition question leads naturally into a question on the same topic that requires analysis, these two questions are placed together. This is so that candidates do not lose their train of thought on the topic whilst answering an unrelated question.

A common problem for students (and teachers) when completing a topic is the lack of examination questions that cover only the topic in question. These questions have been tailored so that students can apply their learning whilst a topic is still fresh in their minds either during the course or when a particular topic has been revised in preparation for the examination.

Questions 1 to 6 are all focused on a specific area of content covered in the same order as in the Content Guidance section of this guide. These questions may be tackled during the course or on completion of the revision of that particular content area. Questions 7 and 8 are, respectively, integrated Marketing and integrated Finance questions for final revision purposes. These could be used together as a final 60-minute mock exam. In the examination you must complete two questions in 60 minutes, so allow 30 minutes to answer all parts of each question.

Sample answers

Resist the temptation to study the answers before you have attempted the questions. In each case (except question 8), the first answer (by Candidate A) is intended to show the type of response that would earn a grade A on that paper. An A grade does not mean perfection — these answers are intended to show the range of responses that can earn high marks. In business studies, it is the quality of the reasoning that is rewarded. With the exception of question 6, candidate B's answers demonstrate responses that warrant a pass, but not at the A-grade level.

Examiner's comments

The examiner's comments are preceded by the icon 🄴. They are interspersed in the answers and indicate where credit is due. In the weaker answers, they also point out areas for improvement, specific problems and common errors such as poor time management, lack of clarity, weak or non-existent development, irrelevance, misinterpretation of the question and mistaken meanings of terms.

Market analysis

Study the information and answer **all** parts of the question that follows.

Under 16s — catering operations

The information below shows the results of research into the 'eating out' habits of one segment of the market — children aged 10 to 15 years. The survey was carried out by 'Mintel'.

Survey data	
Number of children aged 10 to 15 years	4.1 million
Size of sample	584
Type of establishment	**% of sample who have 'eaten out' in this category of restaurant**
Burger restaurant	94
Fish and chip shops	78
Pizza/pasta restaurants	56
Shop/supermarket restaurant	53
Fried chicken restaurant	45
Public houses	43
Chinese	41
Roadside	38
Hotel	23
Curry	22
American theme	18
Other theme	11
Others	48
Don't eat out	5

Other observations
(1) 30% of families eat out 'frequently'.
(2) Burger restaurants are popular because they are 'cheap, quick and palatable'. 5
(3) Children prefer combining 'fun' with food, and value opportunities to carry out other activities whilst visiting places where food is served.
(4) Parents like safe environments for their children.
(5) Children like variety in their food, and are less likely to be brand loyal. They also want entertainment to be available. 10
(6) Pocket money is increasing, leading to more of the older children eating out without their parents. For children choosing to eat out with friends the price is very important.
(7) The results do not meet the '95% confidence level' for statistical significance testing.

Source: *Leisure Management*, November/December 1999.

question

(a) **What is meant by the phrase '95% confidence level'? (line 13)** (2 marks)
(b) **Outline two problems of using primary data to research this market.** (6 marks)
(c) **Examine the benefits of using segmentation analysis in researching the 'catering operations' market.** (8 marks)
(d) **Using the information provided, where appropriate, discuss the chances of opening a successful 'American theme' restaurant in Britain.** (9 marks)

Total: 25 marks

■ ■ ■

Answer to question 1: candidate A

(a) In market research a larger sample will lead to more accuracy in the results. 95% confidence level means that conclusions drawn from the sample should be correct 19 times out of 20.

> *e* A very thorough definition showing a full understanding. The precise use of language has reduced the number of words needed to ensure full marks for the definition.

(b) Collecting primary data is expensive. There is also a danger of bias — the person asking the questions may not ask a representative cross-section of teenagers, thus ignoring the opinions of some sectors of the market. If only older teenagers are asked, then the company may introduce a product that only appeals to that age range. If most people asked are females, then the wishes of males will be ignored, although this would be a good strategy if it was known that only girls ate out.

> *e* Two correct points, but the question asks for two problems to be explained. Given the excellence of the second explanation, a brief development of the first idea on the expense of collection would have secured maximum marks.

(c) Market segmentation means identifying groups of customers who have specific needs. An example of a market segment would be teenagers. A firm can benefit from identifying a market segment because it can make products especially for that group. A theme restaurant based on bands popular with teenagers might be popular, although it may have limited sales if the rest of the population is not interested, as they may be put off eating in such a place.

> *e* An excellent start. Analysis requires 'the development of a line of thought'. The comments on the impact on other (non-teenage) customers demonstrate this skill.

Market segmentation can also be used in gap analysis. This is when a firm uses a grid to see if there is a gap in the market. If a gap for American style restaurants were discovered, then this would support the introduction of these restaurants. However, it may be difficult to be certain that people understand what they are. Only 18% use these restaurants at present, but it is a large and growing market and the firm may have a 'first mover' advantage.

e The argument here combines application and analytical skills, i.e. the comment on gap analysis is then supported by a recognition that it is a largely undeveloped market. Although it is not included in the information provided, it is a valid point. In the exam you will be expected to introduce your own knowledge, if this helps the answer. However, be cautious. A fairly common mistake is to get carried away with showing your knowledge and then to forget the exact wording of the question.

Advertising campaigns can be targeted at certain market segments too. Many firms, such as Pepsi, use famous pop stars or footballers to promote a product in order to increase sales amongst teenagers.

e Further analysis. This argument could have earned application marks if direct reference had been made to its use by an American theme restaurant. However, it would be necessary to make the argument specific to such a restaurant (e.g. a theme of famous rock stars). Application marks have generally proved to be more difficult to obtain than analysis marks on Unit 1, partly because a general argument with the name of the company included is *not* application if the argument could be applied to any firm. Thus adverts based on Eminem would be seen as 'application' if a rap theme restaurant was being promoted, but adverts using David Beckham would not be relevant. (As a general rule, if your argument about the firm applies equally well to a firm that is not involved in the case, then it is analysis rather than application.)

(d) The data show that only 18% of children use American theme restaurants. This would suggest that they would not be successful.

e The information is being used, but only in a basic manner. It appears that the candidate is going through the data, rather than structuring an answer that suits the question.

Burger restaurants attract 94% of all youngsters — this is a very high percentage, especially as 5% do not eat out at all. Fish and chip shops are also very popular, but I do not think that they will increase in popularity and so this would not be a sensible choice. Pizza and pasta restaurants might be a better choice as they are healthier than the other types of restaurant, and the majority of people do use them. The other places are not likely to attract a group of teenagers.

e Although there is relevance in this paragraph, it is dominated by description (rather than analysis) of the statistics, a common tendency in examinations. This answer would have been improved by arguments showing why these trends would help (or hinder) the new American theme restaurant or by the introduction of arguments based on the qualitative information (other observations) too.

Burger restaurants like McDonald's can be found in most places and this is why they are the most popular. Teenagers may not use American theme restaurants because they are not so common as burger places. If a new American theme restaurant was opened, it might be successful, especially if there was not one in that area. It depends on the tastes of the local population.

The final paragraph includes a promising line, based on access to restaurants, but remains undeveloped. The final sentence is an excellent example of how to introduce an evaluative argument, but it is not fully evaluative as it does not state why or how it depends on tastes.

This is a borderline grade A answer. The consistently high standard of the earlier parts means that the (relatively) weaker part (d) would not stop the examiner from awarding an A grade, but to gain an A grade overall this quality would have to be maintained throughout the examinations.

(Note: it is possible to get an A grade in AS with weak evaluation, but application and analytical skills must be displayed consistently.)

■ ▨ ▨

Answer to question 1: candidate B

(a) A firm would be 95% confident that something will happen.

This is too vague. It is advisable to avoid repeating words from a definition question in the answer. The brevity of some student definitions restricts their ability to make their understanding clear.

(b) • Is the sample large enough?
  • The questionnaire — it would be difficult to get the wording right.

A large sample would mean that the results are more reliable. The bigger the sample the better the results and so the business is likely to make better decisions. This will increase productivity and profit, so shareholders can get larger dividends and the share price will increase.

The same benefits will occur if the wording is right in the questionnaire. Questions should be answered by 'Yes' or 'No' so that the data can be processed more easily. Using words that the people answering the question will understand is also important.

The points made are both correct, but the style of development is not ideal since the problems of using primary data are not clearly explained. The first paragraph explains the benefits of a large sample (the problems of a small sample are implied). The second contains separate points. However, the answer does not relate specifically to 'Under 16s — catering operations' and so only limited marks could be awarded.

(c) • Products can be made especially for a particular group of consumers.
  • Adverts can be tailored to the tastes of the market segment.
  • Higher prices can be charged.

This answer only shows knowledge — the lowest skill level. The use of bullet points should be avoided. Only 30% of the AS marks (grade U) are awarded for content/knowledge. This is poor examination technique: there are three good points made, implying that the student does possess further understanding, but the examiner can only reward what is seen. Show your reasoning whenever possible.

(d) I believe that an American theme restaurant would be successful. Only 18% of children eat in this type of restaurant. This may mean that they are unpopular but it also means that there are a lot of opportunities for growth.

At one time Fish and Chip shops dominated but as places like McDonald's and Burger King opened up more shops, the Burger restaurants took over first place. This might apply to American theme restaurants — they are fairly new ideas and may grow.

It would be useful to see a similar survey from 5 years ago — this would show which types of restaurant were growing and which were declining. If American theme restaurants have become a lot more popular in the last 5 years, then this would be a good sign. However, trends do not always continue into the future and so this would not be a guarantee of success in opening a new restaurant.

The sample is not very large. There are 4.1 million children, but only 584 were asked. It is also not clear whether the survey is up to date.

A theme restaurant is ideal for fun, and so this would be a good idea for a restaurant. If the children had to pay additional money for the fun, this would also help the profit. However, this may put off children, especially when they are out with their friends, because they won't want to spend their own money.

With a 'safe environment' it may be better to advertise to families who will be more prepared to pay higher prices and pay more for the entertainment. This is likely to reduce the number of customers, but it could increase profit. Unfortunately, the American theme may limit the variety of meals — this would be a disadvantage.

An exceptional response that earned maximum marks. The suggestions made are developed well and cover a variety of factors and approaches. There is judgement shown: the need to study earlier surveys; the scope for additional revenue from 'fun'; the targeting of families, and the limitations of this approach.

The main strength of the answer is its structure — the information included (quantitative and qualitative) is used to address the question, and the broader implications of some key arguments are included. It appears that the candidate has spent time thinking about the likelihood of opening the restaurant.

This is a grade-C answer. The high standard of the final part allowed the candidate to overcome some earlier problems. There is a tendency for students to leave insufficient time for the final part of the question, even though it carries the highest mark (40% of the total). This candidate left enough time and was able to show depth of understanding in the final part of the answer.

Marketing strategy

Study the information and answer **all** parts of the question that follows.

Cereal makers face crunch as supermarkets go global

The specialist cereals producer, Jordans, is feeling vulnerable — as well it might, with just 2% of the British market. The arrival of Wal-Mart, following the American supermarket's takeover of Asda, is spreading terror amongst Britain's smaller food suppliers. They feel that they will be too small to have any place in supplying the new, global supermarket chains.   5

But global markets also bring opportunities for focused producers such as Jordans, which can operate in a niche market as consumers choose healthier eating and turn their backs on food produced by intensive farming.

Yet if Jordans is to take full advantage of the opportunities, it must expand. Bill Jordan, the founder chairman, says: 'We need to double our market share to 4%. The company must   10
differentiate its products rather than compete on price. We need to sustain advertising to develop consumer demand.' Price competition amongst supermarkets is making it more difficult to achieve added value for its products.

Europe accounts for 25% of company sales, and Jordans is intending to increase this proportion of its sales. The aim is to increase growth without jeopardising what Jordans refers   15
to as the company's 'brand integrity' — its ability to produce tasty and nutritious cereals in an environmentally friendly way. It hopes to differentiate its brand through further innovation.

Initially, Jordans sold its products in health-food shops, but supermarkets now account for the bulk of its sales. As supermarket own labels have become more interested in quality, Jordans has diversified into supplying own-label brands for supermarkets.   20

The company was amongst the first companies to respond to the desire for 'food on the run', through the development of cereal bars. This market is worth £36m a year, with Jordans taking a 35% market share. It has recently moved into the adult savoury snack market with a low-fat cereal-based crisp.

An ability to judge the life cycle of its products has helped Jordans, which anticipated both   25
the decline of the white flour market, and the expansion of healthy foods, in the 1970s. Current concerns are the decline in small retailers and projected long-term patterns in spending. In 1980, British consumers spent 20% of their incomes on food. In 10 years' time this is expected to be 6%.

Adapted from an article by Jane Renton in *The Sunday Times*, 12 March 2000.

(a) Identify *two* of Jordans' marketing objectives stated in the article.   (2 marks)
(b) Explain *two* limitations for a company that operates in a niche market.   (6 marks)

(c) **Analyse how a company such as Jordans might use product differentiation in order to increase sales in a mass market.** (8 marks)

(d) **Evaluate the difficulties faced by a company such as Jordans in trying to predict the length of the stages of a product's life cycle.** (9 marks)

Total: 25 marks

■ ■ ■

Answer to question 2: candidate A

(a) Jordans' marketing objectives were to double its market share and differentiate its products rather than compete on price. It also wanted to sustain its advertising and maintain its brand integrity — its ability to produce tasty and nutritious cereals in an environmentally friendly way. It has also recently moved into the adult savoury snack market.

   e This student starts well by naming two relevant objectives in the first line. Towards the end of the answer the student starts to quote irrelevantly from the text — the focus of the question has been lost. This is not penalised — the student has foregone marks in time wasted. The best approach would be to keep to the instructions (two objectives) when first answering the question, but to leave space in your answer book so that you could return and add further points, if time permitted, towards the end of the exam.

(b) Demand will be limited because you are only selling to a small section of the total market. Jordans aims at 'healthy eaters' and this is why it only has 2% of the market. If it had a mass market product, then it would sell far more and should be able to increase its revenue and its profit. By restricting its potential market in this way it will not be able to reach its target of growing to 4% of the market. It needs to diversify.

   e An excellent explanation, but focusing on only one limitation. The question asked for two limitations. Because of the high quality 'application' of knowledge, it would score more than half marks.

(c) Jordans can differentiate its product by creating a USP (unique selling point). In Jordans' case this is the healthy nature of its products, but it might be achieved through other methods such as advertising or promotion. Branding helps to differentiate products.

   By creating a USP Jordans will attract certain customers who value that particular feature. Jordans will sell to people who want a healthy lifestyle and the more people are convinced that its products are healthiest, the more they will buy. It helps if you are the first to identify the market niche.

   Selling more will mean economies of scale and, with fixed costs being spread over higher output, costs will decrease, allowing Jordans to increase its profit margin or decrease price. This option will make it even more competitive.

Jordans might increase its price, rather than decrease it, because the USP will mean that people will be willing to pay a higher price.

e The development of the USP argument shows very good analysis. The sector on economies of scale also shows analysis. Economies of scale are not within this unit, and so this would not have been required (or expected) by the examiner. However, it is a valid approach and so it receives full credit. The candidate has both applied understanding of business to the case or situation (Jordans in this case) and used theory (analysis). For analytical questions, both application and analysis are required for really high marks.

(d) The product life cycle has four stages — introduction, growth, maturity and decline. All products will eventually go through each of these stages — the aim is to prevent decline as long as possible.

The main difficulty in predicting the stages is the external environment. It is impossible to see the future and therefore companies can only look at the past and make predictions. Often this is a good technique, but trends do not continue forever.

e A very effective start, establishing that the life cycle is understood. The answer progresses logically, showing evidence of sound planning.

It is also not always possible to predict when a market reaches saturation (when no further increase in sales will happen). The potential market for healthy foods might be the whole population, but it may only be a small percentage. Competition is also difficult to predict. If the market grows, will this attract larger companies into the market and so reduce Jordans' life cycle?

Internal factors might also be important — a health scare would lead to decline for any food product, and so the company must keep up its quality. This would be much more serious for Jordans (its reputation is built on quality) than it would be for a different firm.

In conclusion, some stages are easier to predict than others. The introduction period will be decided by the company itself. Maturity and decline will be much harder. Any number of factors — tastes, fashion, competition, the economy — will affect the stages. Companies must be prepared to react as quickly as possible to keep products in the maturity stage, e.g. through extension strategies.

e Putting an argument in context is an excellent way of showing judgement (evaluation). The greater dangers of a health scare to Jordans than other companies is a good example, but overall the quality of evaluation is weaker than the other skills. To some extent too many ideas have been included, which has meant that they have not been expanded in as much detail as would have been desirable. Depth of understanding is more important than breadth of ideas at AS and A-level.

> 🖉 **This is a good A-grade script. All four parts of the question would earn high marks, and this consistency compensates for relatively minor difficulties such as the inclusion of only one point in part (b).**

■ ■ ■

Answer to question 2: candidate B

(a) • To be the market leader.
• To advertise more.

> 🖉 A simple error. Through not reading the question (or not reading the article) the candidate has produced responses that do not answer the question set. The first point (but not the second) shows an understanding of objectives, but does not use an example from the article.

(b) Limited profit. Jordans only sells to a segment of the market and so it will have less revenue than a company (like Kelloggs) that sells to the whole population. The small scale means that it will not be able to compete on price.

Market research problems. Jordans may have limited information on consumers. It might be difficult to identify its particular segment and primary research would be expensive because it may have to ask a lot of customers to achieve a reliable group of healthy eaters. This problem could be eased by targeting health clubs etc.

> 🖉 A very efficient answer: the limitations are noted and the explanations are sufficient to earn additional marks, without becoming irrelevant and time-consuming.

(c) It could use special packaging which consumers would recognise from the adverts or promotions. In this way buyers would not get confused with other, rival products and so sales would rise. Another way might be to use famous personalities, such as Nike which uses famous sports personalities to promote its products. It also has slogans (Just Do It). All of these things help to encourage consumers to buy a company's products as they are reminded that it is different to the alternatives.

> 🖉 This answer is beginning to display a common error. After the initial, brief definition for part (a), the answers for the remaining parts (b), (c) and (d) are of similar length. The mark allocation is an excellent guide to the amount of development required. Furthermore, the three trigger words for question 2 indicate different levels. 'Explain' means apply understanding, 'analyse' requires a further development of the initial explanation and 'evaluate' needs a reasoned judgement to be shown. Consequently, (b), (c) and (d) all demonstrate similar skills (mainly knowledge and application, but little analysis and no evaluation). However, as a percentage of the total marks available, part (b) is excellent whilst (c) is less impressive and (d) is relatively weak.

(d) The stages of the product life cycle would be difficult to predict. Introduction — Jordans would never know when a new product was going to be released because research and development is unpredictable — you never know when a new invention will occur. After that, the stages — growth, maturity and decline — are logical but it is impossible to predict how long each will take. For the computer industry, products can go out of date in months, whilst some foods have lasted for over 60 years. It all depends on the type of product. On balance I think it would be very difficult for Jordans to predict the life cycle.

This classic ending 'On balance I think…' is not evaluation. 'On balance I think…because…' is likely to lead into evaluation if the missing elements are related to the question.

This is a grade-C script. The explanations are generally sound but the ideas have not been developed sufficiently and so analysis is weak. Evaluation is not shown. The student's understanding of basic terms lacks clarity. After part (a) there is not a single factual mistake in the answers, but the candidate's use of short, sharp sentences tends to curtail the expansion of arguments. Factual accuracy should secure a pass at AS, but it will not earn a high grade on its own. In A2 papers this approach would be penalised more fully, as relatively few marks are awarded for knowledge.

Marketing planning

Study the information and answer **all** parts of the question that follows.

Shopping on the go

Home shopping is just the beginning. Grocery retailers may learn to become as mobile as the consumer with convenience being assisted by new technology.

The next big convenience in food retailing is going to be the ability to shop wherever you are and collect wherever you choose. Home delivery is only the beginning of the revolution.

Only the financial services have embraced new technology more than retailers, for whom 5 delivery times and delivery points will be the key. While more of us may be working from home, for those who don't, lifestyle collection points could be where the future is. There are a whole bundle of options out there: schools, corner stores, village pubs to name but a few. With more of the population on the move, stations, airports and bus stations are also prime targets. Transport operators could offer mini-screens in seats, with goods ready for collection 10 at the other end, a system already operating in Holland.

Waitrose looked at stations as a collecting option 3 years ago. Managing Director Mark Price says: 'We explored the option but managing such sites does add significantly to costs.' Research indicates that the price elasticity of demand for many grocery products is very price elastic. Consequently, any option that might increase costs is considered to be too risky. 15

There is nothing restricting shops to traditional store formats. Bristol City Council is considering a proposal that would allow 'park and ride' city centre shoppers to pre-order and then collect their orders from chilled container lorries at the car park.

All of this means a change for marketers too. Retailers will need to strengthen their telephone networks, and advertising and promotion will need to take a different form if the 20 point-of-sale decision is made in a bus or train, rather than in the shop.

Adapted from an article by Belinda Gannaway, *The Grocer*, 19 Februrary 2000.

(a) What is meant by 'promotion'? (2 marks)

(b) Explain two factors that might cause 'shopping on the go' to lead to increases in the price of grocery products. (6 marks)

(c) Analyse possible reasons why the price elasticity of demand for many grocery products is very price elastic. (8 marks)

(d) The article 'Shopping on the go' describes possible future developments in the marketing of grocery products by supermarkets. Discuss the changes to the marketing mix of a supermarket that might arise from the developments described in the article. (9 marks)

Total: 25 marks

Answer to question 3: candidate A

(a) Another word for promotion is advertising, aimed at persuading people to buy your products.

> *e* A simple mistake — advertising is an element of promotion, but promotion is much broader. For AS there are a finite number of terms for definitions and a dictionary is an ideal investment. Accurate understanding can also reduce the chances of irrelevant explanation on the higher mark questions.

(b) Transport costs will be much higher. At the moment manufacturers can deliver in bulk directly to the shops — especially for large supermarkets. A large lorry will not cost twice as much as a lorry half the size. With 'shopping on the go' there will be smaller places where the food is stored, meaning lots more journeys.

Frozen storage will be expensive. Supermarkets have specialist storage facilities in their buildings. In case customers wanted frozen food in amongst their groceries they would have to spend a lot of money on refrigeration.

The technology would cost a fortune. The mini-screens in the seats would get damaged, leading to unhappy customers and high replacement costs. The expense of setting up the system could affect the other activities of the supermarket. They might need to cut back on staffing, leading to low morale and less efficiency and bankruptcy.

> *e* The question requires two factors, but three separate ideas have been presented by the student. In these cases examiners are told to give the mark that would have been gained by the best two (not the first two) ideas. There is no penalty for additional suggestions because the student has lost time, and so will have penalised himself or herself by having to write more briefly later on. (In this example the explanations were clear and so any combination of two factors would have earned full marks — so the candidate wasted time.)

(c) Price elasticity of demand is calculated as follows:

$$\frac{\% \text{ change in quantity demanded}}{\% \text{ change in price}}$$

If the value is greater than 1, the demand is elastic.

> *e* This demonstrates a clear understanding of the term and would earn both the content marks available. Content/knowledge marks can be earned **either** by showing a clear understanding of the topic (elastic demand) **or** by stating the points required (in this case the reasons why demand is elastic).

Competition will affect elasticity — the grocery market is very competitive and so buyers can pick and choose between different suppliers. If you cannot match the prices of other sellers, you will lose a lot of customers. They will want the cheapest goods. This is not always true though. If you can persuade the shoppers that your product is better quality, then they will not always buy the cheapest version of the product. Heinz Baked Beans are still very popular but they are dearer than the shops' 'own label' brands.

Substitutes — if there are many alternatives then it will be dangerous for a supplier to increase its price as customers will buy other products that are similar, but cheaper. Shops will then become reluctant to stock the product if it does not sell — they do not want to waste their shelf space.

Necessity — necessities such as bread will have inelastic demand. However, most grocery products are not absolutely necessary and so the price must be competitive.

> *e* The candidate has secured the content marks by making relevant points and so in this case the initial definition did not help to secure marks. It is good practice to define terms, but not if it prevents you from completing the paper in time. Practice will let you know if you can afford this time. Overall this is a good response, containing logical analysis of ideas that are related well to the grocery market. The lack of development would have prevented all 8 marks being awarded, however.

(d) Clearly 'place' is going to be the main factor. The organisations that can identify and buy the best sites for collection will have a tremendous advantage. At the moment supermarkets charge extra for home delivery and a lot will depend on whether this will become more competitive, like the internet, with charges coming down. For some people time is more important than others. Busy commuters would think this was a good use of their time; others might think it was anti-social — they might enjoy their weekly visit to the supermarket. For this reason I think that it is unlikely that supermarket shopping will disappear.

Price — if the terminals were linked to one company only, it could have the effect of reducing competition. But it would have the opposite effect if you could sit on a train and compare prices of different shops.

Promotion would be less important, or at least need to change. The article states that the point of sale will no longer be in the shops. All of those clever displays designed to make you buy on impulse will no longer work. Of course you can transfer them to the computer screen, but the small size of the new screens will reduce their impact.

This may be a disaster for impulse-buy products too. If people stop visiting shops, will they still be tempted to buy chocolate? It's difficult to see how these products will survive. New ways of promoting the product will be needed. Perhaps they can be displayed at the collection centres. If it is possible to do without the size of shops that currently exist, it will give the supermarkets more money to invest in the new technology and collection centres.

> *e* This is an exceptional answer. The reply has a logical structure based on the key concept required (the marketing mix). Each element is analysed well and some original judgement is shown in the way arguments are extended into long-term

3

implications and 'what if' scenarios. The main strength of the answer is in the way that it is 'rooted' in the situation in the case. Some comments (e.g. those on price and impulse buys) show real insights that could only have arisen from thinking during the exam, as opposed to presenting ideas that had been formed before seeing the questions. The promotion argument also uses suggestions included in the article effectively.

e **This is a high-level grade-A script. The third argument in (b) could have been replaced by more development in (c), but this is a petty criticism. In writing this extensively this candidate earned almost maximum marks, but be cautious. Although this could have been completed in 30 minutes it would be very difficult. Often a really long answer suggests that a candidate has devoted more than 50% of the time to one of the two questions, leading to a weaker second answer. In general, it is sensible to balance your time evenly (unless you do not understand the other question).**

■ ■ ■

Answer to question 3: candidate B

(a) Promotion aims to draw consumers' interest and attention to a product through different forms of communication such as advertising and point-of-sale materials. It can be above-the-line or below-the-line.

e An excellent definition.

(b) Setting up the system will cost a lot of money. New technology is always changing and so you will need to constantly modify and update both the systems and the stock list and prices. Another cost will be payments to other companies. You will need to rent space (although this might be cheaper than your shop). Also the transport operators will want a share of the money.

e A sound answer, directly related to the question and scoring very well.

(c) If demand is price elastic, it means that the quantity demanded will fall a great deal. In order to compete, the firm will have to cut price. This will be good for the firm because it will sell more if it cuts its price and so it will make a bigger profit. If it puts up its price, it will lose all of its customers and go into liquidation. Companies prefer inelastic demand where they can put up their price and still sell the same amount.

e This is a weak answer. The student is listing hazy (often incorrect) recollections, but most critically he or she is not answering the question — factors causing elastic demand are not shown. How many factual errors can you spot? (See p. 55.)

(d) • Product — this will not change. Shops will still want to stock the same range. They may have to stock less if there is no space.

- Price — this will go up to pay for the extra costs of storage and delivery. They will also pay redundancy to the workers in the shops.
- Promotion — they will need to advertise their new service. This might mean that they have to cut back on advertising the actual products that they sell. There could be posters at the bus or train station, or even in the train, to encourage people to use the service.
- Place — both the wholesaler and the retailer will be bypassed.

e This answer demonstrates poor technique. Bullet points encourage brevity and these answers offer only brief explanations. They are also rather general, with little evidence that the candidate has read and understood the article.

e **This is a low D-grade script. However, despite the general lack of depth and the weakness on elasticity, the candidate does show understanding in all of the other areas, but the approach used has led to relatively few marks for the higher skills of analysis and evaluation.**

Factual errors in candidate B's response to (c)

- 'If demand is price elastic, it means that the quantity demanded will fall a great deal.'

e Only if there is an increase in price (by a smaller percentage).

- 'In order to compete, the firm will have to cut price.'

e Not necessarily — in these types of markets firms will use other elements of the marketing mix to avoid a price war.

- '...it will sell more if it cuts its price and so it will make a bigger profit.'

e It will sell more but cut its profit margin and so it might actually reduce its profit. Information on costs would also be needed to draw a conclusion.

- 'If it puts up its price, it will lose all of its customers and go into liquidation.'

e This is too extreme — *some* customers may be lost (and profit may be reduced).

- '...put up their price and still sell the same amount.'

e Inelastic demand means that quantity falls by a smaller percentage than the price increases, but it will not stay the same (unless it is perfectly inelastic).

Question 4

Classification of costs, profit, contribution and breakeven analysis

Study the information and answer **all** parts of the question that follows.

www.intersaver.com

TILL RECEIPT:	TILL RECEIPT:
High Street Electrical Retailer	**www.intersaver.com**

Product: 28″ Toshiba Widescreen TV		Product: 28″ Toshiba Widescreen TV	
Selling price (excluding VAT and delivery costs):	£468.00	Selling price (excluding VAT and delivery costs):	£382.80
Cost of purchase of item (from manufacturer):	£348.00	Cost of purchase of item (from manufacturer):	£348.00
Total overheads allocated:	£42,000.00		
28″ Toshiba Widescreen TVs sold:	1,000 units		
'Thank you for your custom'		'Thank you for your custom'	

Cut out the middle man

When you see the figures on the receipt, it shows how much you can save without the middle man. Intersaver offers you the leading brands at the lowest prices — online or on the high street. By bringing buyers together we give you the muscle to go straight to the manufacturer.

You can compare our prices with the major retailers and, when you've made your choice,   5
all you have to do is sit back and relax while we deliver.

Forget high prices on the high street and remember, there is a better place to shop.

Adapted from an advertisement for **www.intersaver.com**,
published in *The Times*, 17 March 2000.

(a) **What is meant by the term 'overheads'?**   (2 marks)

(b) (i) **Calculate the 'contribution per unit' for each television sold by the High
    Street retailer.**   (3 marks)

   (ii) **Based on the figures in the table, calculate the total profit made by a High
    Street retailer that sells 1,000 Toshiba Widescreen televisions.**   (3 marks)

(c) The High Street retailer wishes to calculate its breakeven quantity for the sales of Toshiba Widescreen televisions. Analyse the difficulties in using breakeven analysis for this purpose. (8 marks)

(d) Discuss possible reasons why the advertised price of the television bought from the High Street retailer might be higher than the advertised price of the television bought through the internet company. (9 marks)

Total: 25 marks

■ ■ ■

Answer to question 4: candidate A

(a) Overheads are indirect costs. They do not arise from the production process, but are needed to support the running of the organisation, regardless of output (e.g. rent).

e An excellent definition worth full marks.

(b) (i) Contribution per unit = selling price – direct/variable costs per unit.
£468 – £348 = £120 per unit.

e Maximum marks again. By showing the working this answer insures against any calculation errors. If there had been an arithmetic error (e.g. £468 – £348 = £130), the answer would have been given 2 out of 3 marks. However, an answer of £130 with no working shown would receive zero because it is wrong and it is impossible to see if it is a minor or major misunderstanding.

(ii) Profit per unit = contribution per unit – overheads per unit = 120 – 42 = 78.
£78 × 1,000 = £78,000.

e Full marks again. It is generally easier to score maximum marks on questions that need calculations than those requiring explanations.

(c) Breakeven analysis is calculated by fixed costs/contribution per unit. The calculations are based on certain assumptions — the selling price and the direct costs are always the same, whatever the level of sales. In practice, this is highly unlikely — to sell more you may need to reduce your price, and so the total revenue would not be a straight line on the graph. The major problem is the fixed costs. A shop will sell more than just one type of television and so the overheads (like the rent) are not just there to sell one product. This makes it impossible to calculate the fixed costs for a particular television.

e Factually good. The candidate gives reasonable explanations and some further development of the lines of argument to reach analysis.

(d) The High Street retailer would have to pay high rent for its premises. Rents in town centres would be much higher than other places. **www.intersaver.com** could have its premises anywhere, and so it would choose the cheapest place for rent.

The High Street retailer also employs a lot of staff to advise and persuade the public. Because there are lots of competitors on the High Street they also need to spend more on promotion and advertising compared to the internet company.

Another important factor is the layout of the store — a good layout might encourage customers who would be willing to pay more (it would also be a more costly overhead for the retailer than **www.intersaver.com**).

> This is a fairly concise response but it is well focused on the question and the candidate applies business ideas to the case very well. Evaluation is shown in the penultimate paragraph, but the candidate fails to evaluate the other ideas. However, the candidate does demonstrate effective use of the information provided — a useful skill in evaluation.

> **This is a good A-grade script. The quality of understanding is high in all five parts. In (c) and (d) it could be argued that some elements are left unsaid. Credit can only be given for the arguments and logic shown — for example, the logic behind the first idea in part (c) is never explained. The candidate states that the total revenue would not be a straight line, but doesn't explain why this is a difficulty in using breakeven analysis.**

◼ ◼ ◼

Answer to question 4: candidate B

(a) Overheads are fixed costs. They do not change.

> There is some accuracy in the definition, but a common mistake has been made. Fixed costs do change (in the long run) but they do not vary with output in the short run.

(b) (i) £468 – £348 – £42 = £68

> The student has confused contribution and profit, and compounded this by making an arithmetic error. However, the working is useful because it shows the thinking behind the calculations and the examiner can assess whether level 1 ('some' under-standing) has been reached.

(ii) Profit = 68
£68 × 1,000 = £68,000

> This apparently wrong answer earns full marks under the 'own figure rule'. The £68 should be £78 but since the candidate will have been penalised for this mistake in (b)(i), the answer which follows on from this is seen to contain no errors of application or arithmetic and earns all 3 marks. The advantage of showing working can be seen here.

(c) Breakeven analysis measures the quantity at which income equals costs. Where total revenue = total costs is the breakeven point. Any sales above this figure are known as the margin of safety.

The firm will need to work out its costs. This may not be easy. Toshiba produces many television sets and so a salesman in the shop will not just be concentrating on one product. Also, the person on the till and the cleaners will be helping all of the organisation's products.

Also you may not produce the same amount as you sell.

e This answer is not addressing the question. Credit is given for the content (breakeven is recognised) but the points made have not been explained sufficiently. This is a pity because the ideas confirm that the candidate probably understands the difficulties, but credit cannot be given for assuming that a student understands something if he or she has not written it down.

(d) The main reason is shown in the till receipt. **www.intersaver.com** does not have to pay overheads. The High Street store's overheads come to £42,000. This accounts for most of the difference. Delivery costs are excluded — these may be cheaper for the High Street retailer.

When people buy from the High Street they are paying for convenience and advice. The shopkeeper can tell you about the product and if something goes wrong, you have a place to go to complain. Customers will pay more for this service and convenience.

Some people don't like to pay on the internet, as their credit card details may not be safe.

e This is a good final answer. In the opening paragraph the candidate uses the information provided to make an immediate, justified evaluation. However, after this the candidate tends towards briefer explanations with some analysis in the middle paragraph.

The final sentence is a sound foundation for further expansion, but a high-quality idea is wasted through lack of explanation (and yet it is hard to imagine that the candidate was not thinking more deeply about the use of credit cards to pay for goods on the internet).

e **Despite some errors and omissions, this answer includes a number of good ideas. The fact that the examiner could see the thinking behind the calculations would help this answer to reach a grade-C standard.**

Company accounts

Study the information and answer **all** parts of the question that follows.

Hillstoke's dilemma

Anthony Kellow, the Managing Director of Hillstoke plc, considered the proposal from his brother, Mark.

Table 1 Cash-flow forecast for new product project (all figures in £000)

	2004	2005	2006	2007
Opening balance	20	(20)	80	30
Income from new product	600	700	750	800
Borrowings/new finance	500	0	0	0
TOTAL CASH	1,120	680	830	830
Purchase of fixed assets	500	0	0	0
Project costs	440	(b)	600	400
Interest payments	200	200	200	200
TOTAL OUTGOINGS	1,140	600	800	600
CLOSING BALANCE	(20)	80	30	230

'This might be the best financial solution,' suggested Mark. 'If we take out the bank loan, we can purchase the fixed assets needed to complete the new product project. But the bank manager did think the project was risky. He also wants the loan to be repaid over the next 5 4 years. However, after 2007 we can expect more income and we won't have the interest payments remaining.'

'But the profit potential is enormous if the new product is successful.' Anthony's sense of frustration was becoming difficult to control. 'Perhaps we should look for other sources of finance. What other suggestions did the bank manager make?' 10

'He suggested that sale and leaseback might be appropriate for the office block: a guaranteed 15-year lease would be possible,' said Mark.

Anthony was uncertain. 'Perhaps there are other sources of finance that we should investigate.'

(a) What is meant by 'sale and leaseback'? (2 marks)

(b) In the cash-flow statement above, work out the missing value for the project costs in 2005. (2 marks)

(c) Anthony believes that 'income from the new product' in 2004 will be 7% higher than Mark's forecast shows. Calculate the new closing balance for 2004. (4 marks)

(d) Examine the perils that Hillstoke plc might face in trying to complete a cash-flow forecast for the project outlined in the article. (8 marks)

(e) Evaluate the different sources of finance that Hillstoke might use in order to fund the fixed assets needed for the new product project. (9 marks)

Total: 25 marks

■ ■ ■

Answer to question 5: candidate A

(a) It is selling your property to another organisation and then renting it back from them. In the end it may cost more money, but its major benefit is that you get a lump sum of money at the start.

> *e* A good definition. The mark scheme requires 'a clear understanding of the term'. This passage more than meets this requirement.

(b) £400,000

> *e* This would earn 2 easy marks. Note that 'subtraction' was the most challenging piece of arithmetic. In business studies it is the logic behind the data that is invariably tested, rather than extensive calculations.

(c) 7% of 600 = 42.   42 + (20) = 22   Closing balance = £22,000

> *e* Another 4 easy marks. Remember figures in brackets are negative and so the extra income has turned a negative cash-flow forecast into a positive one. Remember also to convert your final answer back into £000s.

(d) • It is difficult to predict sales. External factors can change and a recession will mean a drop in income.
  • The costs may change too. If sales were low, Hillstoke would not have to spend so much on wages and raw materials, although fixed costs would not change as they would have been paid already.
  • Interest rates will change.

> *e* Bullet pointed answers are not a good idea. This answer contains three key ideas, and it is obvious that the first two have been understood, rather than just remembered. If the student had expanded on these brief explanations and shown how these points made cash-flow forecasting difficult, the response would have shown 'analysis'. These points do not conclude by showing the 'perils of trying to complete a cash-flow forecast', although all of the relevant ideas are present.

(e) Hillstoke could choose from a variety of sources. It could get a loan. A bank would want security for the loan — the office block must be owned by Hillstoke and so it could offer that as security. The disadvantage is that if it does not pay back the loan, then the building will be sold by the bank and the company will collapse.

It would be easy to budget for a loan as interest payments are fixed, usually. This would be a disadvantage if interest rates were high. The cash flow shows loan repayments of £800,000 over 4 years, for a £500,000 loan. This seems to be very expensive.

Sale and leaseback would give the company a large sum of money. It would depend on the value of the office block. If it was worth less than £500,000, then it would not be enough. If it was worth millions of pounds, then it would be unnecessary. Sale and leaseback should only be used if all of the cash can be used productively. According to the cash flow, Hillstoke will need an overdraft in the first year.

Without further information on the nature of the project it is difficult to advise the company. New products are often risky and so a venture capitalist might be the best bet. If the cash flow is accurate, they could see the benefits of the investment.

> *There is real insight shown here. The opening paragraph shows that the candidate has read and understood the situation, and then been able to apply understanding of business to it. The examiner is now on the candidate's side, eager to award those elusive maximum marks. Evaluation is shown in the comment on interest rates and the identification of the expensive nature of the loan. The fourth and fifth sentences of the third paragraph are also evaluative, and so is the conclusion.*

> **This is a solid A-grade script. There are three outstanding answers, although the brevity of part (d) would prevent the examiner from awarding maximum marks overall. Perfection is not expected (although it is nice to see in an exam) and, even for an A-grade script, there is scope for some errors or weaknesses if your overall understanding is sound.**

■ ■ ■

Answer to question 5: candidate B

(a) Leasing is renting. If a company rented a property, it would be cheaper than buying.

> *The question has been misread. Always double-check that the term is not the one that you wanted to define rather than the one asked for.*

(b) 400

> *Strictly the answer is wrong as it should read £400,000. It is always safer to include the pound sign and the noughts. However, as the wording says 'in the cash-flow statement', 400 would have been allowable in this case.*

(c) £62,000

e No marks out of 4 here as the answer is wrong and there is no working shown. It is probable that the candidate added £42,000 and £20,000, ignoring the minus sign. If this working had been shown, it would have earned 3 out of 4 (for the same answer!) as the correct method could be seen and only a minor error was made.

(d) New products are always unpredictable. In an ideal world the cash-flow forecast would be based on past experience and trends. Trying to predict the fortunes of a new product is very difficult. Even market research will be unreliable as potential consumers may not know whether they will actually buy something. The idea may be promising, but competitors may introduce a better product. This will affect your sales.

Trying to predict costs of new projects always causes problems. The Millennium Dome cost far more than expected and sales were much lower. Of course, if the new product is replacing an existing line, this may be less of a problem. The sales predictions show a steady rise until 2004. This might be optimistic if there is a recession by that time.

Tastes can also change.

The interest payments are £200,000 each year. If a bank loan is not used, then this part of the cash flow will prove to be wrong. If the bank manager thinks it is risky, he may not agree to the loan.

e Excellent analysis, and the example of the Dome helps to illustrate the point. 'Examine' means analyse. Three of the four paragraphs extend the line of thought, but the sentence on tastes (whilst correct) adds nothing to the quality of the answer. You will not be expected to present four different lines of argument. After reading and rereading the passage (time well spent) there should be about 8 minutes for this question.

(e) The best choice would be sale and leaseback. There will be no interest payments to make and if a large enough sum is received, the new product could be researched more effectively. It also provides flexibility — if you do not own the property, you can move to other premises when it suits you.

e 'The best choice' suggests evaluation, but the absence of any other sources of finance negates any suggestion that there has been evaluation here. Marks would nevertheless be awarded for the justification of this source.

e **This script is a borderline C grade. Part (d) is a top A-grade standard and marks have been picked up on the other parts. Time management does not appear to be a strength here — there was probably not enough time for part (e). A second source of finance would have brought this response close to the B-grade boundary.**

Budgeting, cost centres and profit centres

Study the information and answer **all** parts of the question that follows.

Budgeting at Macrohard

At first glance the figures looked fine to Gill Bates, but computer software was her speciality — not departmental budgets.

As the founder of the company she had, at first, been reluctant to delegate authority to other staff. Managers had complained that their innovative projects were being slowed down by Gill's approach.

5

This approach, in Gill's opinion, had been justified by the worrying tendency of teams to acquire huge budgets and then overspend them. On one occasion the company had nearly gone into liquidation, despite increasing sales revenue. She accepted, however, that this reluctance to give authority to other managers had delayed and restricted some new ideas.

The introduction of 'zero budgeting' and 'profit centres' had, she felt, been a key factor in improving the company's financial performance.

10

'Doors 2005' was the name of Macrohard's latest product. It was an innovative piece of software that opened up routes into a variety of alternatives. 'Doors 2005' was the updated version of the 'Doors 2001' system, which had catapulted the company into the public eye. Early signs suggested that 'Doors 2005' would further improve the company's reputation, especially as it had not been upset by the delays and bugs that had been a feature of 'Doors 2001'.

15

Table 1 Budgeted expenditure for 'Doors 2005': financial year ending 31 March 2004 (all figures in £m)

Item of expenditure	Budgeted expenditure	Actual expenditure
Raw materials	14	12
Assembly line wages	15	13
Research & Development	22	28
Marketing	8	4
Other costs	13	13
TOTAL	72	70

(a) **Explain the meaning of 'zero budgeting'. (line 10)** (2 marks)

(b) (i) **Calculate the variance within the budget for 'marketing', indicating whether it is favourable or adverse.** (2 marks)

(ii) **Explain *one* possible reason why the total of actual expenditure did not match the total budgeted expenditure.** (4 marks)

(c) **Analyse how the introduction of 'profit centres' might have helped Macrohard to improve its financial performance.** (8 marks)

(d) **Discuss the problems involved in setting a budget for the 'Doors 2005' project.** (9 marks)

Total: 25 marks

■ ■ ■

Answer to question 6: candidate A

(a) In zero budgeting there is no automatic sum allocated to a budget holder. The manager responsible for a budget must make a case to justify their request for money.

e A precise definition earning maximum marks.

(b) (i) £4m — adverse.

e £4m is correct, but adverse in expenditure budgeting means overspending. This is a favourable variance because it under-spends the budget allocated (although the lack of marketing may cause unfavourable effects).

(ii) They may have cut back on marketing because they had overspent on other items and needed to save money somewhere. They could promote the product more in the following year.

e This is a concise and accurate response, but there is not quite enough explanation for full marks.

(c) A profit centre is a section within a company that has the authority to run itself as if it was a separate business within the company. This would speed up decision-making.

It would also improve decisions — the people spending the money will understand the nature of their business and will be able to take the right decisions, rather than seeking approval from a senior manager with less understanding of the problem. The budget manager will have the incentive to make the right decisions as she will be responsible for any mistakes. The lack of interference will help them to seize new opportunities without the delay caused by having to seek approval.

The disadvantages of 'profit centres' are that they may be difficult to control. If the senior managers give too much freedom, then costly mistakes can be made without them realising it.

There is also a danger of too much freedom — different profit centres may follow similar paths and end up competing with each other, wasting company money by duplicating effort and resources.

In conclusion, Macrohard should use profit centres because the benefits — speed and new ideas — are big advantages in computer software. These companies will always need to take risks.

question

 A very good start to the answer with a brilliant conclusion that relates the concept to the company in the article. However, the answer drifts away from the question in the third and fourth paragraphs by looking at disadvantages, and therefore not showing how profit centres would have helped the company. The candidate has lost time in this section. Balanced arguments, as presented here, are best suited to evaluation questions, although factors that weaken the strength of a case can be analytical.

(d) Firstly, research and development is difficult to judge because unexpected problems may occur. These will lead to unforeseen costs. Testing might reveal further problems, which could not have been predicted.

Doors 2001 had been upset by delays — this would have added to costs.

Good planning would allow for some unexpected spending as plans very rarely go as expected. If a plan did run smoothly, the budget allocated may, looking back, appear to be too generous.

Some costs, like marketing, may be easier to control, but a good budget would have certain targets. External changes (such as more competition) may mean that more marketing is needed if the targets are to be met.

In evaluation, this final factor would be the most important because in a rapidly changing environment the effect of competition and changes in the market could not be guessed. This could be why they overspent on research and development, changing the product to match a rival.

The Doors 2001 project, if it was similar, would have helped to reduce the problem, as they would have gained experience from the budgets for that product.

 A good approach has been used here. By leaving the evaluation to the end, the student is able to bring in the factors that influence the importance of each idea; in effect, the candidate is weighing up the evidence as a judge would do when making a judgement.

 **The consistency of these answers has enabled the candidate to accumulate marks throughout the paper and, despite the occasional hiccup, this response is worth a very solid grade A. Note how, despite this being a financial question, a high mark script is dominated by written comments with very few calculations.**

■ ■ ■

Answer to question 6: candidate B

(a) Zero budgeting — when no budget is given to a department. The department would need to earn the money before they could spend it. There is no automatic right to a budget.

e The final sentence reveals 'some understanding' of zero budgeting and so a mark would have been earned. It is always worth having a go. Examiners want to give credit to people who have 'some' idea.

(b) (i) £8m – £4m = £4m (favourable)

e Full marks for a correct answer.

(ii) The budgeting process may have been at fault. If the managers setting the budget did not understand the item, then they may have budgeted too much or too little money for it. In this case, the actual expenditure could be very different to the budgeted amount.

Wages might be changed. If the company gave a smaller increase in wages than expected, this would affect all departments which may have too much money. Flexible budgeting could lead to the budget being reduced. Of course, it may have been because of more efficiency.

e Two suggestions have been made. Neither appears to be based on information in the stimulus material, which may provide help to the student. However, most 'explain' questions require some application of understanding to the situation in the text and so only limited credit could be given for a general answer of this nature.

(c) • Giving more responsibility to managers.
  • Motivating budget holders.

e Bullet points are not a good approach. The candidate lists two correct ideas, but 2 out of 8 possible marks is the path to a U grade.

(d) The firm may not have enough money. If it is not making any profit, then it would find it difficult to set a budget. A bank loan or share issue might be useful to help it to set a budget. If the company can show a cash-flow forecast that indicates a profit at the end, the bank will give a loan. This will be at a fixed rate of interest and should help the budgeting.

The expenses will be linked to output. Raw materials and wages will vary directly with output and so the more that is produced the more these will cost. If production levels are different to the amount anticipated, then the budgets will be wrong.

e The question has not been read or interpreted correctly. Setting a budget requires future planning, not sources of finance. It appears that the candidate is trying to put in financial concepts that he or she understands. This will not earn marks if it is irrelevant. In a 60-minute examination you will not be able to show all the things that you understand. Accept this and just show what is asked for by the questions.

e **Only the early (low mark) parts have been answered well. The brevity of (c) and errors elsewhere mean that the candidate would have received a U grade. Brief but reasonable explanations in (c) would have led to enough marks to reach a borderline pass (E grade).**

Integrated marketing

Study the information and answer **all** parts of the question that follows.

Woolsery aiming for a new niche?

The Woolsery twins had always been inventive and their passion for computer games had encouraged them to devise their own adventure games. The brothers set up in business on the day they completed their A-levels.

Advertising in *PC Format* magazine produced an excellent response and sales increased steadily. Jim and George felt that direct mail order was the best approach to distribution. A '99% rating' in the magazine's review of their first major game was the catalyst for a massive boom in sales. Within a short time Jim and George were being inundated by telephone calls, asking for the release date of their next game, although some calls registered complaints about technical problems. Jim felt that this would be an excellent way of undertaking market research — **the telephone callers could provide the 'sample'** that he needed to get to understand the market.

Jim carefully noted the details of the comments made by each customer. Whilst George concentrated on developing some new games, Jim pieced together a picture of their typical customers: 'We seem to be appealing to a niche market — 95% are male, 90% are aged 13 to 17, and most express their interests as 'computer games' and 'watching football'.'

After some less successful games Jim had a brain wave: 'We need to devise a new game for each CD-ROM, but include on it further levels of a previous game.' Sales soared as customers saw this package as two games for the price of one; in many cases new customers were tempted to buy the original version of the previous game, further increasing sales and extending the product life cycle of that game. The twins considered this package of two games to be their **unique selling point**, and were surprised that other games producers did not copy the idea.

However, after 5 years George was becoming disillusioned with the business. 'The problem is I am finding it increasingly difficult to relate to our customers' needs, and the product life cycle of our games is so short that I cannot match the speed with which our larger rivals bring out new games. We need to do something that will involve extending the product life cycle of our products.'

(a) **What is meant by the term 'unique selling point'? (line 21)** (2 marks)

(b) **Explain two benefits of niche marketing to Woolsery Products Limited.** (6 marks)

(c) **Analyse the difficulties that may have been caused by Woolsery's choice of sample. (line 10)** (8 marks)

(d) **Evaluate the methods that Woolsery might employ in order to extend its product life cycle.** (9 marks)

Total: 25 marks

Answer to question 7: candidate A

(a) The feature of a product that can be focused on in order to differentiate it from all competition. The feature may be a real difference or one created by marketing.

e Full marks for a precise definition.

(b) A niche market is a small sector of the mass market, such as teenage computer users. If you can match their needs, then you can produce popular products. The twins understood their market niche and so their products captured a large market share (of the niche).

Large suppliers are less interested in small niches and so they are less competitive. This can mean less advertising, saving money. Prices and so profits can be high because there may be no alternatives.

e The candidate makes two distinct points, and explains both well. Careful reading of the case has opened up the first point.

(c) The sample is biased. Jim is only getting information from people who telephone. These are probably extreme opinions — customers with complaints or fans eagerly awaiting the next release. The same person could be included more than once, not reflecting the balance of customers.

Over time, opinions will change. The data seem to be collected over a long time. This would make the opinions unreliable.

The questions are not structured and so the results would be hard to collate. Some pieces of information may not be given by all of the telephone callers.

The data seem to be qualitative — asking people's opinions about Woolsery; this would help them to understand the market.

It is very cheap, except for the phone call charges.

The major problem is that it is all primary research. Jim does not have any information on the market, competitors, and so on. It has helped them to find out the interests of their buyers and given ideas for new products, but it ignores people who do not buy from them. In the end they won't grow without new customers.

e This answer earned maximum marks, but the time the candidate spent on it may have prevented him or her achieving high marks on part (d). The first and last paragraphs both show excellent analysis, and the marks given could have been earned just on these two elements.

The other four points are brief (and the final two are not relevant because they are benefits). At A-level, the quality of the logic matters far more than the quantity of suggestions. There will not be time to explain every possibility — it is better to focus on two (or maybe three) ideas. Both sides of a question are needed for evaluation, but not usually for questions based on analysis or explanation.

(d) Extension strategies should be used.

A price cut will always increase sales. Even the most popular computer games lose popularity and decline, but shops will cut the price to encourage those who won't pay the full price. This should be delayed until Woolsery is sure that its keen buyers have all paid the full price. Teenagers like to have the latest game, and will pay more when it is new.

Special offers — buy one get one free — could help too.

If the only way that you can buy from them is direct mail, then this will restrict sales. Impulse buys will not take place, and customers who might have wanted Woolsery's products would not know about them, especially if Jim and George only advertise in one magazine.

The products must be good, but, on the evidence given, it seems to me that they could increase sales by advertising in other magazines. They should try a magazine that is read instead of *PC Format* — this would make them more well known.

Another strategy would be to contact shops. Shops take a part of your profit but if they help to get the company name noticed, it should help all of the games — not just those approaching the decline stage.

> Another answer of a high standard, with business thinking being used to advise the actual firm in the context of the question. These answers read more effectively than those offering more general advice that could apply to any situation. The third paragraph on 'special offers' could have been developed relevantly but was less likely to have opened up opportunities for evaluation.

> **This candidate gave a well-planned set of responses. In general, the length of development has suited the needs of each question. As the maximum marks available (and skill required) increase, the candidate has extended the depth of his or her response. The only suggestion for improvement is the deletion of some elements of (c) in order to provide more time for (d). This answer is so strong that this candidate would only need to achieve a high E on the accompanying Finance question in order to secure an A grade overall for the Unit 1 paper.**

■ ■ ■

Answer to question 7: candidate B

(a) The unique selling point is the unique feature of a product.

> This is a weak definition that repeats the key word 'unique'. It is essential that a different expression is used to convince the examiner that the term has been genuinely understood.

(b) • The firm can specialise in areas of expertise. For Woolsery Products this means designing computer games for the teenage market which they understand.
   • Higher prices can be charged.
   • Large firms may not be interested in competing because of the size of the market.

e A good opening response. The second point has not been explained and so would earn only 1 mark. However, the examiner would give marks for the best two answers, so the third point (worth 2 marks) would be counted instead. The candidate has wasted valuable time — it is not advisable to give three answers when two are required, but it is worth leaving space to go back if (and only if) time allows at the end of the exam.

(c) The market research is not very scientific in its method. Jim just finds out what customers think from the conversations that he has on the telephone. These customers are a biased sample — only people who feel very strongly are likely to telephone Woolsery. In the article people telephoned to find out about the next game — these would be very keen — not typical of most consumers. The other group were people who complained and so Jim is only getting information from people with strong feelings. The sample is biased because all of the customers read the same magazine. People who read this magazine may not be the only people interested in their games. It is not very likely that the sample is very large if it depends on people phoning the company.

e The answer focuses well on bias within the sample. A particular strength of this candidate is the fact that he or she always tries to relate the answers to the firm in the article — an excellent approach to take wherever possible. The end is weak — the idea is sound but not one that can be developed. Concentration on the narrow segment investigated would be more productive.

(d) The product life cycle can be divided into four stages — introduction, growth, maturity and decline. Sales are very low during introduction as people are brand loyal and will be reluctant to switch to a new product. 90% of new products fail. If the product survives this stage, sales will grow and there should be a lot of advertising at this stage to increase brand awareness. During maturity sales will reach their peak.

e Questions must be read carefully. Although product life cycle is mentioned, this question is about extension strategies — elements of the marketing mix that can be used to prolong the life of a product.

When sales start to decline the business needs to employ extension strategies.

e At this point the answer begins to earn marks.

These strategies will boost sales, preventing the product from going into the decline stage. Extension strategies include cutting price, increasing advertising, modifying the product, and aiming the product at different markets.

question

e Only content (knowledge) marks are earned for the list. This is not analysis or evaluation because no evidence is being provided.

I think that Jim and George should cut the price and aim their product at different market segments.

e The candidate only starts to 'apply' understanding at this point, immediately demonstrating analysis in the final line as the argument is extended in a way that relates to Woolsery. However, it lacks supporting logic.

e **This is a grade-C answer that reflects poor examination technique rather than poor understanding. Answers were applied well, but the lack of development would limit the number of marks that could be awarded.**

Integrated accounting and finance

Study the information and answer **all** parts of the question that follows.

Marje and Joe Ltd

Marje was studying the latest accounts. Things were looking good — most of the debts had been paid off and the shareholders could look forward to a healthy dividend payment. Marje's only concern was the Charles Street warehouse. Customers now wanted immediate delivery, straight from the printing press, and so the warehouse was rarely used for storage any more. Her concentration was broken by Joe as he entered the office. He placed the chart on the desk 5 (see Figure 1).

Figure 1 Costs for new printing press

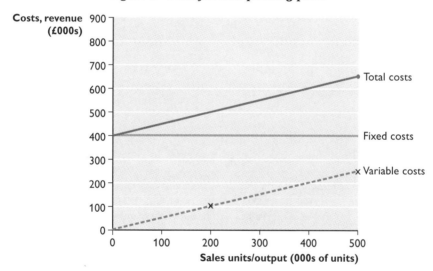

'I've calculated the costs of setting up the new printing press,' announced Joe. 'Fixed costs will be £400,000 per annum and each magazine that we print will have variable costs of 50 pence.'

'Thanks!' replied Marje. 'Our market researchers suggest that we sell the magazines for 10 £1.75 each. At that price we can expect to sell 500,000 copies a year.'

Trish, the Finance Manager, spoke up. 'We should be able to raise the £500,000 that we need from internal sources of finance.'

'What about the day-to-day running of the project?' asked Marje. 'The last project was chaotic and lost us a lot of money. Nobody seemed to know what was going on.' 15

'No problems!' exclaimed Joe, 'Martin is really keen to take on the project.'

8

question

'Right,' said Marje, 'let's go ahead with it. Joe — you, Trish and Martin can meet to agree a budget for the project. Martin can operate the new printing press as a profit centre.'

(a) **What is meant by the term 'variable costs'? (line 8)** (2 marks)

(b) *Either* **calculate the breakeven output for the new printing press** *or* **plot the total (sales) revenue line and show the breakeven output on Figure 2 below.** (4 marks)

(c) **Using a calculation or the breakeven chart, indicate the 'margin of safety' if 500,000 magazines are sold.** (2 marks)

(d) **Analyse two different internal sources of finance that Marje and Joe Ltd might use to finance the project.** (8 marks)

(e) **In relation to the new printing project, discuss the benefits of budgeting to Marje and Joe Ltd.** (9 marks)

Figure 2

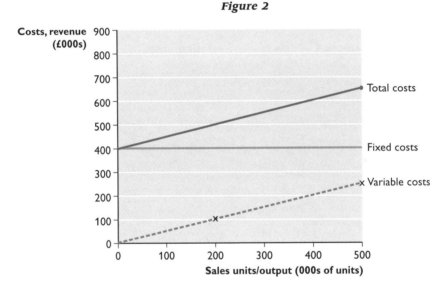

Total: 25 marks

■ ■ ■

Answer to question 8: candidate A

(a) Variable costs are costs that vary directly with output in the short-run.

e Full marks for a correct definition.

(b) Breakeven output = $\dfrac{\text{Fixed costs}}{\text{Contribution per unit}}$

$$\frac{£400,000}{£1.75 - £0.50} = \frac{£400,000}{£1.25} = 320,000 \text{ units}$$

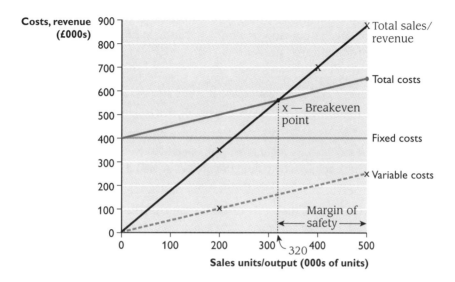

Breakeven output = 320,000 units

e Two correct answers. The question stated **either/or** and so only one approach was needed. In these cases both parts will be marked and the best answer counted, but candidate A has lost valuable time.

(c) According to the graph, the margin of safety is 500,000 minus 320,000 = 180,000 units. It is the difference between the actual output and the breakeven output. Marje and Joe could lose 180,000 units of sales (36% of the output) without making a loss. This is a very good margin of safety as sales are unlikely to fall by that amount.

e Both marks were earned in the opening sentence. Candidate A clearly has a good understanding of margin of safety, but the detail provided was not requested, so valuable time has been lost again.

(d) There are many sources of finance available to Marje and Joe. Internal sources include retained profit, working capital and sale of assets. In the opening line reference is made to the fact that the accounts looked good. This could mean high levels of profit and so it is likely that money could be made available for this new project. Shareholders may be willing to take a lower dividend (there may even be enough profit on top of the dividends being paid, as most firms will not give all of the profit as dividends).

e This is an outstanding opening, showing excellent development of a line of thought (analysis) which is then related to the situation in the article (application).

The Charles Street warehouse could be sold off. There is not much of an opportunity cost involved as it seems to be empty most of the time. It would help the firm to get rid of an unwanted asset and use the funds to buy a valuable and apparently profitable asset, thus increasing overall profit. The article does not say how much the building is worth, but a building is likely to be worth more than a printing press and so this source alone may give Marje and Joe enough money.

e Another excellent example of both application and analysis. These two arguments would merit full marks, so at this point candidate A would have scored **16 out of 16 marks.**

If the firm has good liquidity (again this is implied by the good accounts), it could use some working capital to help fund the project. It would need to be careful not to damage its liquidity (but the text states that it has paid off all its debts).

e Another excellent use of the article to pick up clues to possible answers, but this could have been inserted at the end of the exam, once candidate A was sure that he or she had enough time. It is always sensible to leave spaces at the end of any answer in case you want to return to it to add some more ideas.

As the firm is free of debts and in a good financial position I would advise it to use external sources of finance. Banks would be eager to lend money to such an efficient firm and so it could easily raise the money, using the Charles Street warehouse as collateral security. It could probably get a low interest loan because of its credit rating, and current interest rates are historically low so now would be a good time to borrow.

e Unfortunately candidate A has stopped answering the question set and, even if he or she had not already earned maximum marks by now, this argument would earn no marks. The question expressly asks for internal sources of finance and so external sources earn no credit, however well they have been argued.

The firm could use venture capital, although this is more likely to apply to high risk firms, whereas Marje and Joe Ltd seems to be well established. Shareholders could easily be persuaded to buy more shares, but Marje and Joe may be reluctant to do this as it could give extra voting rights to outsiders, and so Marje and Joe might lose control of the business.

e This has moved further away from the question (although the response could have been retrieved by showing how internal sources would help Marje and Joe to keep control).

e **This is an example of a candidate who wanted to show how much he or she knew on each topic. Consequently, each answer went beyond what was needed to achieve maximum marks and ultimately this meant that there was no time even to attempt part (e), which carried 9 of the 25 marks. Thus despite four well-developed and correct answers, candidate A would have only been awarded a grade B. Although this is an extreme case, many candidates penalise themselves in this way by allowing too little time for the final (high-mark) part.**

Answer to question 8: candidate B

(a) A variable cost is a cost that is not fixed (e.g. raw materials).

> *e* This is not really a definition — the link to output must be included (but the example confirms that the candidate has some understanding, worth 1 mark).

(b)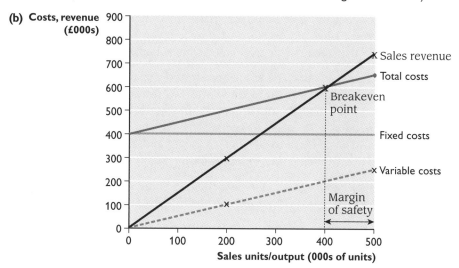

The breakeven point is shown by x and so the breakeven output is 400,000 units.

> *e* The total/sales revenue has been plotted incorrectly (price is £1.50 in this diagram). However, the breakeven point and quantity have then been interpreted correctly and so this would earn some credit under the 'own figure rule'.

(c) The margin of safety is actual output minus breakeven output.
500,000 – 400,000 = 100,000 units.

> *e* Based on the (incorrect) answer to (c), this is perfectly correct and so under the own figure rule it would earn full marks. In this way the candidate is not penalised twice for the same mistake.

(d) There are many sources of finance that a firm can use: bank loans, overdrafts, retained profits, sale of shares, venture capital, sale and leaseback, sale of assets. I would recommend Marje and Joe to get a bank loan as they could easily repay it from the profits they are making. The bank could provide an overdraft for day-to-day expenses.

> *e* This is basically a list of sources of finance, with no distinction between internal and external sources. However, as two internal sources are mentioned, 2 content marks would be given. There would be no other marks as the limited explanations refer to external sources.

(e) Budgeting could benefit Marje and Joe Ltd in a number of ways. A generous budget could show the importance of the project to all of the staff. In particular it could be

a major motivator for Martin who has been given responsibility for this budget. If he is responsible for a profit centre, his rewards could be linked to the performance of the profit centre, providing a lot of motivation for him to do well.

However, it is vital that the budget is realistic as it could be very demoralising for Martin if the budget was too strict. Fortunately, it looks as if three people will decide on the budget and so it is probable that it will be reasonable. However, this would depend on the characters involved — as a junior, Martin may not want to argue with the others and end up with an unsuitable budget.

A major benefit of budgeting is that it assigns responsibility. The last project was a failure because no one seemed to know who was responsible. With clear lines of responsibility for a budget, any unfavourable variances can be linked to the budget holder, making it easier to correct the problem. Constant scrutiny of variances can help the firm to identify problems and strengths, and use this information to improve the efficiency of the business.

By involving senior managers in the budgeting, the firm is guaranteeing that the budget is being used in ways that meet the needs of the firm.

In conclusion, budgeting can bring many benefits, and Marje and Joe seem to have addressed the possible weaknesses of not involving staff in the process. As long as the allocation is reasonable, and flexibility is built in to allow for changes in the internal or external environments, this project should benefit from the budgeting process.

e This is an excellent piece of evaluation. Key benefits are identified and the explanation of every benefit is linked to the situation. This process involves evaluation in its own right, and this is then supported by a balanced conclusion that looks at possible problems of budgeting before making a final judgement.

e **This candidate has an excellent understanding of budgeting, but was weak on all other aspects of the question. However, some marks would have been earned on all of the other parts and overall candidate B would have gained the same mark as candidate A. This would have been a grade-B script too, although candidate A wrote much more knowledgeably and fluently.**

If you are looking for a grade-A script, then combine candidate A's answers for parts (a), (b), (c) and (d), with candidate B's response to part (e). This combination would earn maximum marks.